Migrant Journey to a Marine

Joe T. Rivera Sr.

ISBN: 978-1-5356-1798-7

STORY ONE

Rudy Castillo, Art Renteria, and myself. Vietnam, 1968

The Early Years

I was conceived by a couple of teenagers who fell in love right after World War II in a small town in Mexico. I was born in 1947, J Trinidad Rivera, as my Mexican birth certificate states. However, my dad stated that the J in front of Trinidad stood for José. When I was three my parents decided to immigrate to the United States. My sister and I were left with my grandparents for the next three years. I learned to take care of myself to survive. It seemed that my grandpa spent fifty percent of his time working his land and the other fifty percent drinking it away. So that left my grandma to take care of my sister and no time for me.

The years seemed to just melt away. Then, out of nowhere, there were these two strangers hugging me and giving me new shoes and new clothes. My parents had come back for us. I liked my old clothes better; I wore the traditional white shirt, white pants, and sandals that all of us Mexicans Indians wore.

In 1953 we left Guanajuato, Mexico, to immigrate to the United States. My parents had already experienced the good and bad of being illegal immigrants in the United States, so they didn't want us to go through what they had already gone through. My dad had a plan. He rented a one-bedroom house for us three, my mom, my sister, and me, in Río Bravo, a town just across the border from Texas. Here I was enrolled in school for the next three years.

In those three years my dad worked in the Bracero Program and also as an illegal alien. He saved enough money to get his green card, and then green cards for my mom, my sister, and me. In 1956, all of us crossed the border together with our legal green cards. I recall crossing the border and hearing this strange language I did not understand. Needless to say, I am still struggling with this newfound country and language.

We traveled by bus to Weslaco, Texas. In Weslaco my dad already had a two-bedroom house waiting for us. It was here where I first learned my love for milk. I was enrolled in local grammar school, and even though I had attended three years of school in Mexico, I was placed in the first grade. Every morning before class began the students were given an eight-ounce carton of milk. It was a short stay! My dad was soon offered an opportunity to join a caravan that followed the crops.

We moved to Hanford, Texas, for the carrot season. But the tornado season is what I remember most of that part of Texas. As soon as the seasonal work ended, we traveled from labor camp to labor camp to labor camp. Our mode of travel was in the back of a flat truck with two other families. In Arizona and Oklahoma we picked cotton; in the outskirts of Chicago, asparagus. As soon as one crop ended, we were traveling to the next. In Indiana we were there for the cherry season, and as soon as cherry season ended, it was on to Michigan for the apple season. At the end of apple season, my brother, Juan Jr., was born. As soon as my mom and the baby were able to travel, on we went to another seasonal crop. It was now six of us traveling together; my newborn brother made us five and a newfound friend of Dad's from Texas, José Ochoa, made it six. My dad bought a 1949 Studebaker with suicide doors. Now we had our own wheels. We arrived in Idaho early for the potatoes. As soon as potato season ended, it was on to California for the grapes.

What made those early years so great and unforgettable were the events that occurred in each labor camp.

The labor camp in Illinois was made up of two rows of one-bedroom homes with a centralized community shower and bathroom. We kids spent our time shooting marbles and taking walks out away from the camp. During one of our walks, our parents got worried and one of them went out in his pickup to bring us back. We were about two miles out, on our way back. But he would not let us walk back. So we climbed into the bed of the pickup. Just as the pickup started to move, I dropped my comic magazine. Without thinking, I automatically jumped out to get it. I was holding on to the tailgate but the truck started picking up speed. I let go of the tailgate and slid on the dirt road and started rolling. The driver could not see me so he just kept going.

I was hurting. I had scratches and small rocks embedded in my arm. I picked up my magazine and walked all the way home crying. The first person I encountered at the camp was my mother. She started to yell at me and at the same time was hugging me while taking out the small rocks embedded in my arm. I felt so stupid but I had my magazine. Finally the asparagus season ended and it was on to another labor camp.

In Indiana, the labor camp was in the middle of the cherry orchards. Here we were allowed to help our parents pick cherries. Once again we lived in a one-bedroom house. The first thing that got my attention was that the kids were not playing but working. I made picking cherries into a game.

After work everyone just sat around talking instead of playing. Most of the conversation was about girls. One of the girls' names that seemed to be spoken about more often was Lupita. *Who in the hell is this Lupita?* I wondered. A week later all my questions were answered. I never got involved in the conversations. I had no input; I just listened. In the middle of one of the discussions, everyone stopped talking and started toward a group of women. In the middle of these ladies was the most beautiful girl in the world. Someone pointed toward her and identified her as Lupita. I fell in love at ten years old. As the group of ladies passed by, Lupita and I locked eyes. I could not utter a word; I just stared at her. As she looked at me, I could see a smile. She was twelve but looked much older. Someone noticed me looking and commented that she was too old for me. I could never get enough courage to talk to her. All I managed was a simple hello with a smile. I would think to myself, next time!

And then the worst thing that could happen happened. My dad and I were picking cherries on the last tree for the day. I asked my dad permission to go to the bathroom. Before he answered, I ran; I had to go bad. I could hear him yelling to be careful. I ran into the first clump of bushes I came to and squatted. In my haste to relieve myself I'd forgotten the toilet paper that we carried for such occasions, so I just pulled leaves from the closest bush and that was that. At least I thought it was. That evening my butt started itching. I had never felt that way before and I did not attend the usual gossip session. By the next morning, I felt blisters and the itching was worse. I explained the situation to my mother. She made me pull my pants down so she could see. She yelled and called Dad over. My dad knew what it was. He called me a few choice names I had not heard before: "Pendejo [stupid], you clean yourself with poison ivy!"

I was taken to the nearest medical facility. Because of the location of the infected area, the blisters were burned out with a laser. Because of my limited English, I was confused. My mother was given instructions through an interpreter. I've always wondered if there was anyone else as stupid as me! At least the itch had gone away.

I asked my mom not to tell anyone about my problem. But the gossip had already passed throughout the labor camp. That night I got my first get-well wishes as I lay on my stomach. I could see Lupita. She asked to see me. She stood there next to me. She put her hands on me and told me how sorry she was. I could see tears coming down her face. I just couldn't say anything. She was also saying goodbye; they were leaving for another labor camp. She asked why I would not talk to her! She touched me again and said goodbye, turned, and then Lupita was gone. I don't know that at ten years old you are supposed to feel this way. I felt like my heart was going to burst, but I also felt ashamed that it happened in this way! As she left, she turned to look at me one more time and gave me a smile. Time has no consciousness, it just moves on and on. So did we the traveling migrants, traveling from harvest to harvest.

We moved on to Michigan for the apple harvest. I don't know how it was arranged, but we were left at an apple ranch. The rancher welcomed us with open arms. I couldn't believe it; no more labor camp. We were housed at an actual two-bedroom home with a shower, bathroom, and stove, all in one house. My mother was super happy. She was expecting her fifth child, my brother. My parents had lost two baby girls to illness while they were working as illegal aliens. I did not think much about it since not much was said on their births or deaths.

I was looking forward to climbing those beautiful apple trees and picking their beautiful red apples. It was short-lived excitement. My parents explained to my sister, Estela, and me that here we were to attend school. We were enrolled in a country schoolroom that taught about twenty students from kindergarten to twelfth grade. It was my first exposure to snow. The school was about a mile away from the ranch and with no bus transportation, we walked to and from school every day. My mother gave birth to my brother, which increased the family to five. Once again the harvest ended and it was time to move on. The rancher liked my dad's work ethic and asked him to stay on. But plans had already been made to follow the crops, so my dad had to decline his offer. However, he promised to return the following year.

With the help of the rancher, we bought our first family auto, the 1949 Studebaker. We loaded the car with all our belongings and moved on to Idaho. A friend of my dad's joined us on the long trip. Now there were two drivers to share the driving. I am still in awe that we undertook traveling through five states and about two thousand miles and made it in one piece. We stopped for gas, for groceries, and to use the bathroom. Our diet consisted of bologna sandwiches, potato chips, and soft drinks. I had no sense of time, so I just enjoyed the long ride across our United States.

After about a week we arrived in Idaho. It did not look like anyone was busy working. It was still winter and everyone must have been inside their homes. Upon our arrival we were informed that we were too early for the harvest and that there was no work or living quarters. However, we were directed to a one-bedroom shithole, a cabin where we could stay until harvest. An empty cabin with a fireplace. The fireplace served as heater and stove. We had to live off the land for food and also for the wood for heat and cooking. I spent all the time helping my dad, hunting, fishing, and gathering wood. With my dad's survival instincts we survived that cold, cold winter. He took me out searching for our food. We searched and found wild roots for vegetables. We trapped rabbits and fished for our meats. We used a diaper pin (safety pin) for a fish hook. A small creek ran near our cabin, which was our main source of drinking water and fish for food.

Anyway, when we'd immigrated to the US I was nine. In Mexico I had finished the third grade and was going to begin the fourth grade. However, since I could not speak English, I was placed in first grade at the Weslaco, Texas, grammar school. So by the time that I began high school as a freshman I was sixteen years old. I competed in three main sports in high school: football, wrestling, and track. I was a two-year varsity letterman in wrestling. I did not attend my senior year of high school but chose to attend full time junior college and take two night courses in my high school diploma. I graduated six months ahead of my 1967 high school. I was too old to compete in high school sports my senior year. A wrestling scholarship up to Cal Poly, San Luis, was waiting for me. I just could not keep my grades up.

After one semester at college and a high school diploma I decided to enlist in the US Marine Corps. My parents were completely against it. The Vietnam War was constantly on the news. Some of schoolmates were getting killed in Vietnam. Since I was the oldest in the family my parents were scared for me. My parents had left my dad's parents, my grandparents, to care for me until I was six years old that here. I was nineteen but we had only been together as a family for ten years. They did not want to lose me again. However, having been on my own for so many years taught me to be independent. My dad did not show much emotion like my mother. But years later my sister told me that there were times that she would see my dad holding my picture and crying. There are things in life that we don't understand or feel until we become parents. One is the love we hold for our kids. The emotional pain that we cause without knowing. I was wounded February 1, 1967, and because there were thousands of wounded and killed that month, the Department of Defense could not identify them all.

There were some events that occurred during my three months at recruit training that, for better or worse, I will always carry with me. I would never want to change what makes a Marine. We are only human and we process events differently. As for me, I found recruit training physically demanding but manageable. From my childhood in Mexico to working with my parents in the grape, orange, cotton, cherry, and apple fields, I learned that the only thing you can control is you and your mind and that there is no substitute for hard work.

On one of our many formations, a private dropped his M14 rifle, the drill instructor (DI) order the private to stretch his arms out with his palms down. The rifle was center on his arms. The private was ordered not to move or drop the rifle. His body shook, sweat poured down his face, but he never dropped his rifle. We were dismissed, but he stayed at attention holding his rifle.

On another formation while we were at attention, I stuck my thumb out without thinking. The DI grabbed my thumb and bent it and asked if I wanted my thumb. At attention your arm and hand is straight down with your thumb pointing straight down next to your forefinger. Both of us privates learned self-discipline and never fucked up like that again.

The last month of recruit training was at Marine Corps Recruit Depot San Diego (MCRD). We recruits were in our last phase of becoming Marines. We were one, a team. We were up at five thirty (0530) every morning and in bed by ten PM (2200), with a good night to Chesty Puller. We were ordered to say goodnight to Chesty Puller: "GOOD NIGHT CHESTY PULLER WHERE YOU'RE AT!" The days duplicated each other, spent marching with our rifles and without our rifles.

We were also allowed to practice our faith. And for some of us, this allowed us to rest and get a little more sleep. I didn't know if the drill instructors were religious or, if so, what religion they practiced. But one Sunday morning a drill instructor on duty sent us to morning Catholic Mass late. One of the recruits was assigned to march us to church. We knew that we were going there late, but we thought that the Mass had been moved with us. We marched back. The private in charge of details reported to the drill instructor. A couple of minutes later he came back and instructed us to return to our barracks and that the drill instructor would come in and talk to us in a few minutes. We were dismissed to our barracks.

The barracks were empty, which seemed strange. And within minutes there he was, our drill instructor, larger than life, dressed as a Catholic church priest. Before anyone could say anything, he started holding Catholic Mass. But we could not make out what he was saying. We just kept quiet and listened to this fool make a fool of himself. We stared at him as he made the sign of the cross and blessed us. Only he knew what he was saying. We just stared at him in disbelief. The only one that was feeling the moment was our drill instructor. Finally, he muttered some words, smirking, turned around, and left the barracks.

To this day, I have no idea what the DI's motivation was. He left a negative impression on us young recruits. We stayed silent for a few minutes after the DI's departure. The silence was broken when someone called for a meeting that night. We met that night and we all agreed that the DI needed to pay for his insult of our religion. We made a pact that we were going to take a shot at him if we saw him in Vietnam. I don't recall who came up with the idea or if anyone actually took a shot at him in Vietnam. However, I have always wondered if anyone actually went through with it. I did run into a few of the guys but no one ran into or knew of him.

A few weeks before graduation, a private from Chicago, a reservist, and I were ordered to report to the senior drill instructor. We looked at each and ran to his quarters. When the gunny brown, the senior drill instructor, called, you listened. We reported in and we were ordered to stand at ease. He stared at us for a minute or so and then addressed us as maggots. He went on to say that he didn't know why, but we had both been selected to attend Navy Shipman School at Quantico[A1] . It was the first step toward becoming Marine Corps officers.

We got orders upon our graduation from recruit training. The only thing that the private from Chicago and I had in common was that we had the highest two scores in physical fitness in the series. I don't even recall how many platoons were in a series. We were in Platoon 2016. I was assigned to communications wire and recall his Military Occupation field (MOS)[A2] . I never received the orders to the Navy Shipman School[A3] . It is what it is, and you go with what life brings you. Life gave me Vietnam in place of midshipman school!

I reported for recruit training, or boot camp, on June 29, 1967. I graduated from MCRD San Diego at the end of September and reported to Communication School, ______ [A4] Training.

Until we were properly identified, we were identified as missing in action (MIA). After getting wounded the first time[A5] , I was medevaced by helicopter to Doma[A6] , New Jersey. After surgery I was transported again by helicopter to a hospital ship, the *Repose*. During my recovery, I was ordered to write a letter to my mother. Apparently, my parents had been notified by a Marine Corps recruiter that I was missing in action.

It took the military two weeks to locate me and notify my parents that I was wounded but doing well!

Not able to walk for two weeks and just lying there gave me a lot of thinking time. The first thing that came into my mind was, "How in the hell did it come to this!" Mexico, then Texas, USA, then high school and a semester at Reedley Junior College, and then the Marine Corps. My so-called girlfriend eloped while I was in boot camp.

Wiremen School in Camp Pendleton went by quickly. Infantry training went by a little more slowly. We were being prepared for combat in Vietnam. Some of the unforgettable events were climbing Mount Mother-Fucker, survival training, the low crawl under live machine-gun fire, and the booby-trapped trail with a Vietnamese village.

Mount Mother-Fucker, now that's a hill for you! I heard that hill called by other names but one thing remains the same, that it's straight up for five miles. We walked it in formation as a company. I was in the last platoon, the last Marine. Everyone walked while I ran to stay up. By the time we got to the top I must have swallowed most of that fucking mountain's dust! You sweated your ass off going up it and you ran down proud and yelling as a conquering hero. You never forgot Mount Mother-Fucker! Go fuck you, all the good, the bad, and the old!

Survival training lasted several days with an indoctrination. We got in bleachers in the middle of a forest. Then the shit started; an old Marine with broken English started shouting and telling us to shut the fuck up. In order to survive in combat, you lived off the land. We were shown different wild vegetables. I don't even remember what they were, so fuck that! The instructor got our full attention. He got a chicken out and swung it around and broke its neck. He skinned it of feathers and skin and started eating it! He did the same thing to a rabbit, and yes he spun it and ate it raw! At nightfall we were given a cup of rice, which was suppose to sustain us. We were placed in a simulated prisoner camp. We were to escape and find our way back to our friendly lines. We took the exercise as a game. We split off in three, four, or five to a group, or a squad, per se. It was not a test; it was a learning tool. By morning we all made it to the designated area. As for the rice, I threw it away. I tasted the rice just to remind myself to never get captured.

The low crawl was a bitch. We had to crawl fifty yards under barbed wire with our rifles. We were instructed that live machine-gun fire was being fired. We were advised several times to not sit up! It felt like there were live rounds going over me. I'll leave it there! We all looked like mudpuppies, covered with mud from head to boots!

We had a class on booby traps. We walked to an area where booby traps were already set up. As we walked the booby-trapped trail to a Vietnamese village—back then we would call it a "gook village"— someone would trip a booby trap or an ambush would occur. The Vietnamese village was full of traps and our goal was to stay alive. This exercise is surreal now, because in Vietnam, we lost many to booby traps and ambushes. I am fortunate that I am still around to talk about it.

Next thing I knew, the fun and games were over. Now it was time for Vietnam and the waiting began. It was the last of November and the Infantry Training Regiment was smack in the middle of Camp Pendleton. It was commonly called Main Side. Everyone knew where we were going but no one talked about it. We were on a twenty-four-hour standby. The telephone booths were a sea of green. We were all calling home to say our last goodbyes. After a week and a half of false alarms, we got the call.

Now it was the first week in December and we loaded onto Greyhound buses. Our sea bags were sent separately in trucks. Once on the buses we were informed that we were headed to Norton Air Force Base, Sacramento area. On the way there we made a stop at the Fresno Greyhound bus depot and it was only a block from where I had enlisted in the Corps. While there I kept hoping to recognize someone. All I could do was look around and say my final goodbyes in my mind! There were hundreds of Marines and civilians around but I felt so alone.

We arrived in the middle of the night at the air force base. We were manifested and herded to the airplanes waiting for us. We were flown to Okinawa, Japan, with a stop in Alaska. Once in Okinawa we had another week to wait before Vietnam. We got additional immunization shots and our sea bags were tagged and stored in warehouses. In the middle of December we were herded into trucks, taken to Futenma Air Station, and flown to Vietnam.

On the way there I had my final nightmare of what Vietnam was like. I dreamed of shooting it out with the Viet Cong and kicking ass. I was crawling and shooting as bullets were flying over my head. I felt like I was winning the war by myself and then I woke as we were about to land in Vietnam.

Vietnam

I don't recall the actual day that I arrived in country. But it wasn't what I imagined it was going to be like. I thought that there were going to be bullets and bombs going off everywhere. Thank God that it didn't happen that way, since none of us had weapons to defend ourselves.

As we stepped out of the airplane there were military personnel everywhere. There was no sign that a war was going on. There were a few catcalls—"Hey newbies, welcome to Vietnam, only 390 days to go." Some were busy having a hamburger and Coke and some just carrying on without a care in the world. I looked around with surprise and amazement. I thought to myself, "This is war?"

We received our orders. A group of us were ordered to board a truck and taken to 5th Marines regimental headquarters. We were placed in a tent that billeted twenty Marines. They were to be attached to 1st Battalion, 5th Marines. I was told that I would join my platoon in a week. The first week was indoctrination. A black corporal was in charge of us. He taught us how to dig a trench hole. How to listen for incoming mortar, yell "incoming" as soon as we heard it to sound an alarm that we were being attacked, and run to the nearest hold or bunker. We were instructed in the art of filling sandbags. I also learned to play different card games like rummy, Hearts, bridge, etc. Rumors were passed on. Some of the stories sounded believable but you took everything with a grain of salt.

I was finally transported to 1st Battalion, 5th Marines, H & M5 Company[A7] , communications platoon, wire section. My platoon commander was Captain Duncan and my wire chief, or platoon sergeant, was Sergeant Bart. I did not get the opportunity to meet either one of them until New Year's.

The battalion had just returned from an operation called Operation Swift. The 1st Bn, 5th Mar had moved on to a place called Phu Loc province, which, I was informed, was next to the bastion border. I was to follow in a few weeks. I stayed in the rear with the gear. As scuttlebutt had it, our camp was located south of Danang and in the middle of nowhere! The camp was going to be taken over by the ROK Marines, a hard-ass South Korean company of Marines. We were instructed to let them take whatever they wanted, and if they happened to take anything of ours to let them take it and they would replace it! As sure as shit, the ROK Marines would walk right through our tents like they lived there. Sure as hell, they took it and replaced it. Isn't that some weird shit or what. So the word was, don't fuck with ROK Marines. We were also told that if they received any type of incoming fire, the assumed area would be destroyed.

One night we heard a shot fired that sounded like it came from one of the security bunkers. Our first thought was that it was the VC proving[A8] our lines or an accidental discharge, which happens. However, we were told that was not the case. Apparently one of the ROK Marines fell asleep on watch and was shot and killed by the sergeant of the guard. How is that for military discipline? None of us witnessed the killing, so you just store it in your memory bank and fuck it!

I spent Christmas of 1967 on security watch. I looked up to the stars and thought of home and family. It was short-lived. I could hear the sound of machine-gun fire at a distance; back to reality.

Just before New Year's we Marines that remained behind loaded the remainder of the regiment's gear onto trucks and moved out to Phu Loei province. The caravan of trucks moved out at 0600. I don't know how many trucks and jeeps moved out. I know that there had to be over twenty vehicles. On route, one of the trucks hit a booby trap, which caused the column to come to a standstill. The damaged truck was moved to the side and we moved on. We were traveling on a one-way road that led up through Hai Van Pass. The trail was steep, narrow, and very cold. I was informed by another Marine that we were traveling through Hai Van Pass; I had no idea what area, he was referring to. I was too cold to care at the time and the only information I got, "Stop" and "Go!". I do recall that there were four of us Marines sitting in the back of the truck. I was wishing that I was somewhere else! The convoy traveled at a slow pace for fear of road mines and the muddy road. We had no pack, no rifle, and not even a field jacket. We were carrying about a hundred M16 rifles, stacked in the middle of the truck bed. We were supposed to be taking care of the rifles. All the bolts had been removed; they were non-operational.

Why the weapons were there, I don't know. I do know that I froze my ass for several days in back of that fucking deuce and a half. What lesson did I learn from that experience? Not a fucking thing, or maybe that I was stupid to take that cold and not say anything. By now, I had been in country for one Christmas, associated with ROK Marines, and nearly froze my ass off, and I still had no idea what the fuck I was doing!

All of the 1st Battalion, 5th Marines companies were based here at Phu Loch. The camp was given a name but I don't recall it. The letter companies operated on constant patrol away from Camp Incoming. Camp Incoming is as good a name as any. The camp was surrounded by mountains, where we were sitting ducks for constant incoming mortars. We had the four letter companies (Alpha, Bravo, Charlie, and Delta) and headquarters and headquarters support (H&HS). I was attached to H&HS, communications platoon, wire section. My platoon commander was Captain Duncan and platoon sergeant was Sergeant Bart. We were tasked with land communication; however, it was an impossible job. We wired up Camp Incoming for inter-camp communication. We put up telephone poles with telephone lines. We had the camp looking like a city. But it was all for nothing; after the first mortar there were breaks throughout the wire system, and all that wire had to be replaced in order to regain communication. So we buried the wire, but we encountered the same problem after another mortar attack. Anyway, it was a mess. There were fourteen of us wiremen with little to do. However, because we still had a switchboard that had radio relay lines attached, which allowed us to contact the outside world, and we also had radio (PRC-25) for communication, we became security and radio operators. We also took turns on switchboard watch and night patrols. I don't how other wiremen in other units did. I only did one tour in Vietnam and that was with 1st Battalion, 5th Marines.

I'd had to spend Christmas of 1967 in Vietnam on guard duty, I had endured the coldest ride of my life, and now I was in Phu Loch for the new year of 1968. At least here I had a rifle and an M16 to call my own. There were a lot of lives lost to constant mortar attacks. We had incoming mortars morning, noon, and night. The month of January was a deadly month. I guess the Vietnamese were giving us a taste of what was to come: the Tet Offensive, Feb. 1, 1968—the Vietnamese New Year, a presumptive ceasefire.

5th Marines Regiment Camp. Over 100 casualties by 2 am on February 1st. I took this the morning of Christmas '67.

16

I never thought how I was going to react when bullets started flying on the flight to this fucking country. Do I miss it? No. Can I forget it? No. I miss Vietnam like the last turd I flushed down the toilet. On my first guard duty assignment I shared it with another fellow wireman. He claimed to be from Tennessee and was very proud of his home state. We were supposed to schedule our watch to two on and two off, where one slept for two hours while the other watched for two hours. Young Tennessee was about six foot four, Super Gun__ [A11] and a picture Marine. Anyway, at about midnight the sky lit up and about five to seven clicks from us it looked like the 4th of July. The VC were attacking a village or another compound. A couple of minutes into that attack we got attacked. Rounds started flying at us. Just then my whole body started to shake and I couldn't control my body. So Tennessee instructed me to smoke a cigarette. He said, light it, cup it in your hand, kneel down, smoke it, and you will be alright. While he was returning fire, I followed his instructions. It calmed me down. I never imagined that this was going to be my reaction on my first firefight! I guess I was scared shitless. Anyone it was the first and last time I reacted that way. Yes, we became the best of friends; I miss him. We remained on alert all morning.

On the following morning our platoon commander, Captain Duncan, informed the communications platoon that the reason we could not send aid to whoever was being attacked was that we had no communication with them and all roads leading to that area were blocked. We were also under attack. He asked for volunteers to accompany him to see if we could render any assistance. We led out of the compound with two small trucks. There were eight of us in one vehicle and I don't know how many on the other truck. We were instructed to lock and load our M16s and be on the lookout for snipers, road mines, and booby traps. We traveled about seven clicks out.

It was a bumpy, beautiful ride. The area was a dense jungle with lots of brush and banana trees. As we got closer to the designated area burnt places started to appear. Then there it was; all the buildings were burned down and it was spotted with dark areas where mortars had hit and exploded. We exited our trucks and searched the area but there was no one around. Within minutes we were instructed to board the trucks and return to base. This area was populated, or had been, by a community action unit that was there to help and aid the local villagers. It was made up military advisors and ARVN (Army of the Republic of Vietnam) soldiers. What happened to the locals and advisors, we didn't know. They weren't there, but as for the VC (Viet Cong), they were celebrating somewhere in the jungle by resting and getting back their energy to strike and kill again at night.

We were back in the compound by the afternoon and in time for supper, our first meal of the day! Through January there were constant mortar attacks. There was no set time for mortar attacks. Sometimes you would be walking for lunch and hear a yell: "INCOMING!" You fell to the ground right there or jumped in the nearest trench. I recall four separate attacks that caused a death. The first was when I was scared shitless! One of the mortars that came on us landed on a Marine in a trench and killed him. The second was in the middle of the day. About forty yards from our communications area two tents had been put up as our dining area. Someone had taken the time and built park tables with benches as our dining tables. Some Marines were walking to lunch and a yell went out: "INCOMING!" As the incoming yell came everyone fled. I had C-rats so I wasn't planning on visiting the dining facility. These three Marines said, "Fuck it, we are going to eat." One mortar came in and it landed on the corner of the table where they were sitting and killed all three. When we checked out the table, there were just spots of blood but hardly any damage to the table. The third time, a week later, I met up with a chicano from Texas. We exchanged names and spoke about those three Marines that been killed. He said that he was a corporal and that he was the regimental sergeant major's driver. He pointed to his tent, where he billeted with the sergeant major. We shook hands and agreed to talk some more another day. We had incoming that night, another couple mortars looking to take lives. Sure as shit, the word went out that the mortars had hit the regimental sergeant major's hooch and had killed both in their sleep! It was just about the end of January. Someone should have come to the simple conclusion that the incoming were not only killing but proving[A12] . Someone on those hills was watching and spotting the shots. Just a guess! The gossip turn to the month of February and the Vietnamese New Year.

We were informed that a ceasefire had been negotiated for February 1, 1968. I don't recall what day it was on January 31 of 1968, but it was nice and warm. It was like a Sunday fun-day. A couple of us wiremen walked over to the other side of the compound and crossed our perimeter wire. A small creek of water came flowing from the mountain and there some Marines sunbathing on the rocks. Some were attempting to bathe and some just sat around talking. Upon our arrival someone shouted to watch out for the small two-step snake. I asked what the fuck a two-step snake was and someone answered that the snake was small, thin, and green, and when it bit you and you took two steps the venom would set in and the poison would drop you dead! It was a picture-perfect day.

It was getting late and we had to return for afternoon formation. Captain Duncan had scheduled a formation and we didn't ask why; we just showed up. All communications platoon soldiers were present. He made it clear that even though a ceasefire had been called, he wanted us ready and prepared for the worst. All lights were to be out at sundown and heavy fog was expected. The formation was short and to the point. As soon as we were dismissed the sergeant called me and told me that the captain wanted to talk to me. The communications area was on a slope. Our living quarters were tents located a few feet from the perimeter wire and in between we had built bunkers. The bunkers were the safe haven from incoming mortars. The captain lived in a one-man tent above our radio-relay and switchboard bunker. Our compound had been occupied by the French army, who had left the manmade brick bunkers in good condition, like they'd left in a hurry. We were told that the French had gotten their asses kicked on the ground that we stood on. Anyway, Sergeant Bart took me to see the captain, who was waiting for us inside the communications bunker.

Sergeant Bart spoke first and said that I was scheduled for switchboard duty and my watch would start at 2000 (eight PM) until I was relieved. I just stood there and listened. Then the captain spoke.

"I want you to keep your ears open. As soon as you think you hear any kind of incoming, wake me up."

"Yes, sir."

So I started the watch as ordered. It was foggy as hell and there wasn't a sound. It was spooky silent, so I kept going outside the bunker to listen. I kept wondering what Captain knew that he wasn't saying. Then at about 0100 (one AM) it happened. I couldn't see anything but I could hear some gunfire and mortar. So I woke the captain up and he'd heard what I heard. He told me to get Sergeant Bart. I brought Sergeant Bart and the firing seemed closer. The captain had taken over for me and gave me an order to wake everyone up and send them to the bunker with rifles and ammunition. So I went from tent to tent and gave the order that the captain had given me. And just like that all shit broke loose. There were mortars hitting everywhere, and then the small arms started; mortar, rifle, and machine-gun fire was everywhere. Because of the thick fog you could only hear and not see it. It stopped for a minute and then it started all over again. It went on all morning and all day.

"Corpsman up!" was a steady call all morning. Every time there was an injured Marine a Navy corpsman was called. The Navy corpsman is a combat Marine's Florence Nightingale. The Navy corpsman heals the Marine and fights alongside the Marine.

Just as quick as the attack started it stopped. We fucked up and decided to leave our bunker and look around. It seemed like it only was seconds that we were outside and I took a step toward my bunker and then all hell broke loose again. I was about two feet from my bunker and one of mortars hit behind me. It felt like fire burning my lower back and my legs. At the same time a few feet from me another Marine was bent over in pain. Out of nowhere the Navy corpsman was next to me and was asking where was I hit. I told him not to worry about me but to check on the other Marine. The way he was bent over I thought he was hit in the stomach area. I felt a terrible burn on the right side of my family jewels. *Oh shit*, I thought, *they got my balls.* I placed my hand down there and my hand came out bloody but they were still there. The corpsman shot me up with a morphine injection and all the pain left my body. But now I couldn't move.

I was taken to a bunker for further first aid, safety, and comfort, but no further aid was administered. The bunker was filled with the dead and wounded, and all morning more wounded and dead Marines were brought in. Unable to move, all I could do was look and observe. Every once in a while I would doze off. I recall two different Marines that were brought in with different outcomes. One Marine I thought was going to die any second; he was bleeding from separate wounds, his feet almost cut off and bleeding, and he lived. The second looked like there was nothing wrong with him and all of a sudden he started gasping for air and just like that he was dead. I was helpless and all this time, there was no cease to their attack on our compound.

Late that morning we were informed that helicopters were on their way to medevac the dead and wounded to Danang. It was estimated that we had around one hundred casualties. Two landing zones (LZs) were set, a primary and secondary. Just about noon two of us wounded were placed in a small vehicle called a mule. The dead were stacked separately. I was on a mule in about the middle of the caravan. I couldn't move my legs and I didn't know if it was from the morphine or if I was paralyzed. Either way, I couldn't feel or move my lower body.

All of a sudden the sound of helicopters was in the air. I looked to where the sound was coming from and I said to myself, *thank God!* Just as the helicopters were circulating to land, the middle helicopter was shot down. The fucking VC started attacking us again. Next thing I knew, everyone was in the trenches and I was left on the mule. I could see mortars coming closer and closer. It was as if they were walking them purposefully toward me. So I started yelling, "Help me, get me out of here!" It seemed like an eternity, but two Marines, a black and a white, picked me up and threw me into a trench. As they ran the mortars started exploding all around. Both Marines that saved my life were wounded. I knew they were wounded because they were bleeding on me. I probably got hit again but I couldn't feel anything. As soon as the attack stopped, we were loaded back onto the mules and transported to the secondary LZ. Just as we arrived, the helicopters landed. First all the Marines killed in action (KIAs) were piled up to make room for all the wounded. By that afternoon I was with hundreds of other wounded lying on gurneys on the runway. We were tagged; a yellow tag was tied to our person with our full name, serial number, date, and branch of service. I looked left and I looked right; I couldn't see the end of the wounded.

I must have passed out or fallen asleep. Next think I knew, I was in this hangar. It was filled with wounded on tables and people I assumed were doctors. I heard someone yelling in pain. Next I heard someone say, "Hold him tight, we are out of anesthetic." The person that was yelling was two tables away from me. I didn't know what to think. All of a sudden the medical staff was around me. I was told to hold on tight and a couple of the medical staff held me down. I felt myself getting cut and I yelled, "Why me, God!" The pain must have knocked me out, because when I woke up I was all bandaged up. I had never felt that kind of pain before and I don't wish that on anyone. However, this was war, and in war there is pain and suffering.

My lower body was still painful. But now I was assured I would be walking in no time. A bigwig came and pinned a Purple Heart on us. To this day, I have no idea who he was. Fuck it! The wounded in my ward called me Speedy Gonzales because it took me about ten minutes to walk to the bathroom or shower. When I reached the shower or bathroom it would take me another couple of minutes to step over a step that had been built between the living area and the shower and bathroom.

Two weeks into being the guest of the hospital ship *Repose*, I ask if all the shrapnel had been removed and the simple answer was "no." I had stitches in two sides of my left calf and in both buttocks. I had a hole in my right inner thigh about an inch from my family jewels. The injury on my inner thigh took longer to heal. The shrapnel had penetrated about six inches into my thigh; it had to heal from the inside out. It was cleaned twice a day; a solution was placed at the tip of an eight-inch cotton swab and it was cleaned out like if you were cleaning an ear canal. After a week of having cotton-swab cleaning, I felt a tingling sensation, as opposed to pain. As for my calf, it was drained for about a week, and then I had stitches placed. Thank the Lord and the Virgin Mary who kept watch over me.

I look back to Vietnam and the thirty days I stayed in the hospital ship *Repose* and wonder in disbelief that it really happened.

Once the strength therapy was complete and my strength returned, I started walking, and I felt strong enough to return to duty. But it was not my choice to make. Nonetheless, I was put to work. My job was the elevator operator. The ship had three or four floors and I just spent the day going up, stop, down, stop, and yes sir, yes ma'am, no sir, no ma'am. My free time I spent reading Western books like Zane Gray and walking on the deck of the ship. If it wasn't for war and my injuries, I would have felt like I was in sea heaven! Like with all good things, something happens to bring you back to reality. On one of my deck walks, I heard a gasping sound and it scared the shit out of me. The sound took me back to the regimental compound at Phu Loc. I followed the noise; it was coming from an intensive care room. I peeked through the upper deck window and there was a soldier struggling to breathe and several doctors taking care of him. He started to gasp for air and just like that he died. I made it my business to find out what caused his death. He died from malaria.

Joe T. Rivera Sr.

The ship made a stop for repairs in the Naval Base Subic Bay in the Philippines and we were allowed to go on liberty. Our liberty stay in town depended on our rank. As a private first class, I had to be back by midnight. We all had a good time. How good, I'd rather not say. But what I do remember is Shit River and the enlisted club on base. You had to cross a river to get from the base to the town, Olongapole, and that river looked like shit and was extremely filthy. Just the same, sailors and other visitors enjoyed throwing coins in the river and seeing the young poor kids dive for the coins. Most of the military personnel seemed to take it as entertainment! I could hardly walk but I made it to town. But lack of cash and strength kept me on the base. So I became an enlisted-club-goer.

On the ship, I encountered and befriended other wounded warriors. Over the years I have forgotten their names, but their images are forever implanted in my brain. On ship we kept ourselves busy by playing card games, talking about home, and reading. I don't recall that we ever spoke about the war and the units that we were attached to.

On the last day in February we were informed that the following day we were going to reach the coastal waters of Vietnam. My orders to return to full duty were ready. I still had stitches in my left leg.

As I waited for my orders and transportation back to mainland Vietnam, a helicopter kept on transporting more wounded to the *Repose*. The Tet Offensive was in full swing. The North Vietnam Army (NVA) and the Viet Cong were invading all of South Vietnam. Helicopters were transporting in the wounded by the dozen. I kept looking and sometimes started hoping that I would recognize someone from my unit. I just wanted a little information on my unit's whereabouts and the health and well-being of my friends in the communications platoon, wire section. I was to be released that afternoon and I finally stopped looking. I started walking toward the Marine Liaison to pick up my orders. Since I'd come with nothing, I was leaving with just my orders and a small bag.

As I started walking, I heard a faint voice saying, "Rivera, Rivera." I thought I was hearing things. No—it was Captain Duncan, lying on a gurney. I just stared at him and it took me a minute to come to my senses.

I said, "Oh fuck, Captain," and I almost started crying. He could hardly speak but he asked me to get close. I said, "Yes, sir," and grabbed his hand. "What happened, sir?"

He said that a sniper had shot him in the throat but that he would be all right. He whispered that he was glad to see that I was OK. Just like the captain, thinking of his troops first. I told him that I was OK and that I was on my way back to the platoon. He said that after I was medevaced out the attack had continued. He said the compound was continuously attacked day and night. Also that the roads and trails leaving the compound were secure.

The NVA and snipers kept the regiment pinned down. The commanding officers of 1st Battalion, 5th Marines went out in a jeep with a small convoy of Marines in trucks but only got about one hundred yards out before they were ambushed. Most of the Marines in the convoy were killed. With the commanding officers' permission Captain Duncan also took out a squad, made up of several from the communications platoon. But he ran into heavy fire. He said that he and several other wiremen were wounded and were repelled back to the compound. He said that a sniper had shot him in the throat area. One of the Marines dragged him back to the compound. He said the Marine's name but I don't remember it. He said that from the hospital ship, he was going to be transported home. Also that the regiment, what was left of it, had been ordered to Hue City. He asked me to let the communications platoon know that he loved them all and wished us a safe return home. He was pushed away and all I could do was stare. I held my tears back and waved goodbye to him.

I met up with my unit in Phu Bai. The communications platoon, wire section, was all split up, the majority headed up to the Battle of

Hue City. Since I still had stitches, guard duty and working parties was the order of the day for me. We were in the same encampment with the Army's 101st and 82nd Airborne. We shared the fight in Hue City and the fun at the same enlisted club. The enlisted club was a big barn that probably held about a thousand Marines, soldiers, and Navy personnel. Beer and soda pop were the only drinks sold. Beer was twenty-five cents and I don't remember what the soda pop sold for. The choice of beer was Ballantine, Lucky Lager, or Schlitz. The club was a sea of green with everyone doing their own thing. There were six to eight to a table. At some tables they were playing card games, at others singing country or Motown, like the Temps and Otis. We were all kids, away from home, trying to forget the war for one evening.

While in Phu Bai I was placed on a thirty-day guard duty. I moved into a tent located minutes from the perimeter. We were paired two to a bunker, on a two-hour up and two-hour down schedule. Just before sundown we set our day more mind out, one left, one right and one in the middle whisk would cover all frontal probably attack[A14] . The corporal would check on us a couple of times a night. One of the biggest points we were instructed on was that there was to be no accidental firing of a weapon. If we fired a weapon then we'd better have a dead body to show for wasting good ammunition. The thirty days just went on by. We were on a rotation basis with one day on and one day off. I don't know how the day bunk watch was scheduled. I was only scheduled for nights.

Every so often the VC would attack us with mortars and rockets at night. When such attacks occurred, we were all sent to a large bunker for protection and to wait for further orders. On one of these attacks we were all talking bull to kill the time. One Marine claimed that he liked incoming attacks because that was when he made fast cash. He was a corporal who claimed to be from Los Angeles and said that during attacks he would people [A15] for a price. He had a different price depending on the area of the wound. I still have the image of him but it's better to leave it there. He also mentioned the race that he was cutting but it's better to leave it there. You have to remember that we were only human and the drive of survival was very powerful.

One of the times that I was relieving the day watch, I saw this clear plastic bag of cigarettes. So I picked it up and yelled at the two guards that we had relieved, "Hey, are these cigarettes yours?" They looked at each other and then at me and one ran back and grabbed the plastic bag of cigarettes out of my hand and thanked me. The following day I shared the story with another guard and got my answer as to why the outgoing guards had acted so strangely about a simple cigarette claim. The plastic bag held not cigarettes but rolled marijuana. Marijuana could be bought for a dollar a cigarette, or ten to a baggie for ten dollars. The rolled-up cigarettes were sold by children or vendors.

There are stories that the rats got as large as cats. I never encountered any rats. But on one of the nights on guard duty, I witnessed a rabbit hopping along the barbed wire on the perimeter line in front of the bunker. To this day, whoever I have shared this story with says that what I saw was a large rat and not a rabbit. I stand firm; I know what I saw, and I witnessed a rabbit!

And just like that, I was back in Phu Bai with my unit. The Battle for Hue City was coming to an end. The Viet Cong kept us well occupied in Phu Bai; rockets were being fired on a daily basis. The problem was that there was no set time. The only sure thing was that they were going to be fired and they were going to be fired in a walking motion. The smartest thing that we had done was to build trenches in front of all our living quarters, which were tents. We did have an alarm system in place. Upon an attack a fire-alarm whistle would blow, similar to the one used in World War II. One of the most memorable attacks that I recall happen one mid-afternoon. Because we never knew when an attack would occur we wore our boots 24/7 and aired our feet out every so often. On this particular day, I decided to stand down. It was a hot, humid day and I put on issued camouflage shorts and lay down shirtless. But I kept my boots on. Just as I started to relax, the incoming whistle alarm went off and the rockets started hitting. The rockets kept getting closer and closer to my immediate area. As the alarm sounded, I was up and running to the trench in front of my tent. I swear that I jumped up and before my boots hit the dirt I had taken several steps in the air. As fast as I thought I had reacted, everyone else had beaten me to the trenches. I jumped into the nearest spot that gave me cover. As long as I was below ground level I would be OK, because when the mortars and rockets hit, the shrapnel goes up in a comb[A16] . The problem was that if they hit on top of you, you were dead.

As the rockets kept getting closer and closer I kept praying and praying. The rocket were hitting so close that the dirt and rocks were starting to hit my naked back. I prayed every prayer that I could remember and asked for forgiveness. I thought that one more and the next was going to land on top of me. But it was not to be so. The attack stopped as quickly as it started. Was I scared, fucking-A!

Now it was the end of April and the Battle of Hue City was over. Most of the talk surrounded Hue City and battle encounters. The Viet Cong and the North Vietnamese Army fought to the death. In some cases they had no choice, because Viet Cong were found chained to their machine guns. So they had no choice but to fight till their death. It was door-to-door fighting similar to World War II. One house and one sheat [A17] at a time. All three regimental battalions, 1st, 2nd, and 3rd, were in the fight along with the Army's 101st and 82nd Airborne. The 11th Marines Artillery Battery was the supporting artillery unit.

Now we the 5th Marines were given another assignment. We were assigned the security force to keep Highway One safe. I was detached outside of Phu Bai. It was the 1st Battalion, 5th Marines headquarters compound. It was a small compound that housed the commanding office, the sergeant major's tent, a headquarters tent, and a security force. I was part of the security force and communications. My sleeping quarters was my poncho held up by two sticks, which made my home sweet home the ground. A poncho liner spread on the dirt served as my bed. The poncho was lightweight, easy to carry; it kept the sun and rain out. On some occasions the poncho kept me warm and dry!

At my rank level, I was given orders and I followed them. As it was well understood in the Corps, "Yours is not to reason why but to do or die!" Here we were in the middle of nowhere without a particular place to go, except going out on listing posts as scheduled. During morning formations we were given assignments. On a listing post, two of us were assigned and just before sundown we were given our final orders. Our M16s were locked and loaded. We carried a radio (PEC-25) for communication. The radio was set to a frequency that only the command center radio tuned into. The communication was a two-way, but only one spoke. Every hour the command would contact us as we held the handset to our ear. The command was, if everything was clear, click your handset once, and if it was not, click your handset twice and return and listen for instructions. We walked about a click out away from the compound. We never used the same trial twice. Once we reached an area about a click away, we split the watch, two hours up and two hours down. The senior Marine set the watch standard. Just before sunup, we started walking back, taking a different trail. Sometimes I scared myself. Lying in the middle of a rice paddy waiting for Mr. VC or Mr. Charlie to appear put my imagination to work. There were times when I saw the grass sway to and fro and thought that all of a sudden someone was going to appear and come at me, or I thought I heard or saw someone out there, but it was just the grass moving to the wind! Yes, I was scared, but that helped me stay awake and vigilant. Four separate outposts were sent out every night. Having security watch was just another extension of the Marines' standards. And it is, but that's one of the lowest times I had in Vietnam. If we were not assigned elsewhere, here we were on the perimeter. We had bunkers and trenches all around the camp. We were protecting the commanding officer of the 1st Battalion, 5th Marines, a central command tent, the radio relay structure, and its staff.

The sergeant of the guard was called Sergeant Flames. As the scuttlebutt went, he'd had a flamethrower squad but it had disbanded and he was left without a squad. He pushed his rank around. He was looking for a way to get to us and I gave it to him and he got me! While we were on watch, he would sneak behind us and try to catch us sleeping or messing around. He wanted us to play Marine and challenge him with "Halt, who goes there?" just like guard duty back in the world. He was so noisy that even the gooks clicks away probably heard him. To make the night go more quickly, we scheduled our watch to four hours on and four off. One of those nights I saw him coming to my left. He got to my bunker and I looked at him and he asked why I didn't challenge him. I said, "I saw you coming and I know who you are." My mistake was arguing with him and not respecting his rank. He said I must have been asleep and that was why I didn't challenge him. I told him to fuck off and get the fuck out. He said he was going to write me up and left. I should have just shut up. But I called him an asshole. The following day he took me before the commanding officer. He had written me up for sleeping on post. I explained to the CO what had happened. He said he knew about the sergeant but still continued with office hour the punishment filling sandbags. But still had I was filling sandbags for to pull guard duty. [A18] I celebrated my twenty-first birthday filling sandbags. Two weeks later I was informed that the incident had been thrown out like it never happened. I sure filled a lot of sandbags. I was still scheduled for night watch. What the reason for all that was, hell if I know!

My third assignment was in the central command tent as the switchboard operator. This was the COC, or the command and control center for 1st Battalion, 5th Marines. The movements and objectives of four infantry companies (Alpha, Bravo, Charlie, and Delta Companies) were monitored along with those of the ENEMY, the Viet Cong and the National Vietnamese Army. We had radio relay with an antenna, which allowed communication with the central command in Danang, set up by the communications platoon, radio and wire section. We ran communication wire from the radio relay van to a frame position outside to the switchboard inside the command tent. To the switchboard and the switchboard as name an SB-22. [A19] The radio relay also made it possible for a wide range of radio communication. Working inside the central command tent gave me firsthand look at combat from the outside, as it happened!

I looked forward to working in the command tent so much that I alway reported thirty minutes early. One of these happy days turned out to be one miserable-ass day. I was assigned to cemetery security for one day. The next thing I knew I was in a jeep with my M16 heading to a cemetery. Apparently the Viet Cong used burial holes and coffins to hide communications and weapons, so several of us Marines were assigned to ensure that no ammunition or weapons were hidden. Some of the families were moving their deceased loved ones elsewhere. We were there to search the holes and caskets as they dug them up and moved them.

It was hot and humid as hell. So I shed my utility jacket and in no time my upper body got darker than I already was. I was standing there sweating buckets, wishing for some sort of relief. I was standing next to a gravesite and some of the locals kept approaching me and talking to me. I had no idea what the hell they were saying. All I could do was stare at them and nod. We were looking in graves and coffins for hidden ammo or weapons and they didn't like it. I commented to another guard that I didn't know why they kept coming to speak to me. The other guard commented that I was short and dark like them and probably thought that I was Vietnamese working with American military. This detail made out to be a long, hot, sweaty day.

A couple of days later we were informed that there was a regimental-sized NVA force coming our way. We were placed on alert. Late that morning a force recon platoon entered our compound. And that afternoon a Navy chaplain held a Mass and after the Mass, we all kneeled and were blessed. Again I was placed on watch; I was assigned as switchboard operator in the central command tent. Now we just waited for the attack. I could hear all the chatter coming over the radio. There was some erratic firing but no sustained fire. The radio relay allowed us to hear what units were under attack and in the middle of firefights. On the following day the fighting increased but it never got to us. Food was plentiful; we were never short of A-rations and heat taps! By the following afternoon the fighting increased and we could hear as the exchange of fire got closer. We monitored some of the radio transmissions between squads, platoons, and companies as firefights were going on. On one particular transmission the firing was intense and then there was silence. The silence broke and someone said, "Be aware that we have a prisoner." Silence; a shot could be heard; and next came more silence. Then a radio transmission broke the silence, with a gurgling and just two words: "Prisoner dead." We looked at each other with a smile. It went silent for a couple seconds and then we just continued as we were. Two days later an all-clear was given. Apparently the regimental force that was coming toward us was nowhere to be found. The enemy had disappeared in plain sight. The following day we packed up and returned to Phu Bai.

Later that week a late platoon formation was called. We didn't even come to attention; we were ordered to stay at ease. Then the so-called good news was given: the entire battalion was moving to An Hoa, which was closer to Danang. The heavy was, since all the support comes from Danang, we would be able to get all the supply support we needed.

First an advance group was going to be sent in to prepare the camp. An advance volunteer group was being formed and volunteers were needed. It was also made clear that there were not enough volunteers and some were given orders to go fulfill the need. I volunteered without giving it a second thought. I recalled last year when I'd stayed in the rear with the gear. I recalled sitting on the back of a truck, freezing my ass off. The convoy moved slowly and here we were to fly in a C-130, a cargo airplane, to An Hoa—why not?

We were instructed to take only the essentials: rifle, ammo, socks, towel rations. We placed the rest of our belongings in our duffle bag, tagging it with our name. On the following morning we took our duffle bags to a designated area to be sent to An Hoa. From the wire section there were two of us that volunteered, Lance Corporal Gates and me. We were instructed to manifest on the runway. There was chaos at the runway. We were placed with the headquarters personnel. We spent all morning on standby. We were dressed up in full combat gear with no place to go. It was hot and humid. By noon we were not only hot but hungry. Someone found several crates with bananas. Now at least we had food, bananas. Some Marines started playing catch with the bananas and so we were ordered to stop and prepare for the flight. And finally at about two PM, we were ordered to line up and prepare to board. It was hard to hear commands given the noise from the C-130s; there were more than two. I did know that I was going to be on one of the cargo planes.

We were all lined up and when the order came to board there was a sea of Marines boarding. I thought to myself, "Where are we all going to fit?" The answer came as we started to board. We sat facing the back door for a quick exit. We sat on the floor, asshole to belly button. My question was answered. Here I was sitting asshole to belly button with pack and rifle. We were instructed to be ready to move upon the arrival at the land strip in An Hoa. I was looking forward to kicking back and preparing the camp for the battalion. It was a short flight to An Hoa and as we were landing the strip was under mortar attack. Then the last thing that anyone thought could happen, happened. As I was sitting at the bar drinking 7 and 7s, waiting for my flight back to hell.

As we were landing at Danang Airport, I recalled that there were a couple of Marines from home that I needed to visit.

[A20] I reported back at the airport liaison and inquired about Red Beach. I told them that I had two friends from home that were stationed there and that I wanted to visit them. I boarded a convoy that was headed there. Art was a motor-T driver with 11th Motors at Red Beach. Don was with intelligence work in Message Center. Art was easy to find and he took me to the area where Don was working. Don was asleep; he worked the night shift. All I could get was a hi and a smile from him so I just left him alone. Art showed me Red Beach. We spent all afternoon and night partying at an enlisted club. We fell asleep out in the open all fucked up, talking about home. Right after midnight an alarm was sounded that the area was being hit with rockets.

As soon as I returned from Arizona Valley I was asked if I wanted to go on a rest and relaxation (R&R) morale leave. I didn't have to be asked twice. So I replied, hell yes. I didn't ask where; I just asked when. My orders would be ready the following day and my departure would be the following week for Tapai, Taiwan, the Republic of Red China. I picked up my orders and traveled by convoy to Danang. In Danang I found myself with others that were going on R&R. I didn't really care. I was glad that I was getting away from hell for a little while. It was seven days in Taiwan for me, while others were travelling to Hawaii, Bangkok, Japan, and Australia, and some were staying in country at Red Beach. I was told to take only enough money to spend for seven days. I took six hundred dollars with me and yes, I spent six hundred dollars. Whatever amount of cash you took you spent.

The flight was scheduled for the following day, which gave me that afternoon and night to relax and get cleaned up. I made friends with a couple of Marines who were also traveling to Taipei. We decided to go to the PX and purchase soap, toothpaste, deodorant, and something to shave with. On the way back to the barracks, we stopped at the seven-day store and purchased some spirits to pass the night. The PX areas resembled all the military PXs. Instead of shopping, we did a lot of staring. I walked toward where this sweet smell was coming from and as I was walking there, I smelled something that smelled like a skunk. I said to myself, *What the fuck stinks?* So I took a smell test, and started smelling myself. *Oh fuck, it's me.* No wonder some of these people were avoiding us. We made our purchase and got the fuck out of dodge.

On the way back we started making fun of each other and how bad we stank. We finally said fuck it and broke up laughing at ourselves. One of the guys wanted to know what we should buy to party. We agreed on Schlitz, rum, and Coke to go with the rum. In the front of the seven-day store a sign read *Liquor Sold to Army, Navy, and Air Force, Not to Marines! A Marine must be a staff NCO and above.* We bought some beer and partied on.

The next day we boarded a flight to Taipei, Taiwan. Upon our arrival, we were given an orientation on how we should conduct ourselves. We were instructed to proceed to the enlisted club and we could get a taxi to transport us to the hotel of our choice. At the enlisted club I sat at the bar and ordered Bacardi with 7 Up [A21] at ten cents a mixed drink. I was starting on my third drink when a taxi driver came in looking for customers. I took the first driver that offered his service. He didn't want any payment; the hotel covered his pay. I gave him a couple of bucks anyway.

The hotel was first class. The one bag I had was carried for me. As I was registering I was asked if I needed a girl to keep me company and I said no. I just wanted to shit, shower, and rest. The bellboy carried my bag and the key to the room. The room had a king-size bed. The bed had call buttons on each side. Anything that I desired was at my fingertips. At the touch of a button I could order any meal, drink, or companion. Here I was, my first time away from home, twenty [A22] years old and living like a king.

I shat, showered, and shaved and asked to have my dirty utilities cleaned. I took the elevator down to the lobby, where taxi drivers were offering their services. The next thing I knew I was in the backseat of a taxi, enjoying being alive! The taxi stopped in front of a nightclub with blinking lights. The club was popping, two ladies for every one male. The taxi driver took me to the person in charge. She looked at me and smiled and asked me what girl did I want. All I could say was "What?!" She walked me over to the bar and lined up about fifteen ladies and told me to pick the one I wanted. So I followed orders and looked. I thought I was dreaming and that all of a sudden I was going to wake up.

Anyway, I finally picked the girl I wanted. She filled out a contract; I paid her. The mamason also wanted it understood that she wanted me to be happy. She said if I wasn't happy with her, to bring her back for another, and if I wanted two, I could take another one. She was on rental for a week. Upon my return to the hotel, I had to pay a twenty-dollar fee for her staying with me. As my escort, she took me to all of Taipei nightlife. We visit the finest restaurants and shows in the city. I didn't understand a word of what was said. But I was treated like a king as if I belonged there. Next thing I knew, I was back at the same enlisted club where my unforgettable dream had started.

Started 3/14/16
II

[A23] All of a sudden the C-130 came to a quick stop and the back door slowly opened. We were told to stand up and double-time out. As we came out, we were directed to helicopters waiting for our unit. Man, it was a noisy morning. We just moved to every command. I believe that most had no clue as to where we were or where we were going. As I looked out of one of the helicopter windows, I could see another helicopter that resembled a snake. I started hearing faint firing and then all shit broke loose. There was nothing we could do; we were just along for the ride. The gunmen on our helicopter joined the gunfight and then we saw the lead helicopter as it was going down. The whole convoy of helicopters circled and then came back around and landed on a rice field. The rear door opened and we ran out as instructed to the nearest dike and dropped to the ground. The area was filled with white smoke for cover.

A yell came: "GAS!" Just then I started choking and I used my towel as protection from the gas. The gas burned the shit out of my eyes and my nose started dripping. Luckily the wind created by the helicopters' propellers moved the smoke out. Yes, I and a few others had screwed up and not packed our gas masks, having been told that what we left behind was to follow us at a later time. Before our departure from Phu Bai, we were told to pack light and ensure that we had a canteen with water, rifle, ammo clips, ammo, towel, and socks. There sure was no mention that we were going to be packed like sardines and then later upon arrival to An Hoa we were going to be loaded in helicopters with no idea of our final destination.

Out of nowhere a second lieutenant started shouting orders. Our target destination was the banana plantation fifty yards to our front. We ran and dropped, ran and dropped. It seemed like an eternity in time but it only took minutes. We made camp in the middle of the banana plantation. The word was passed to dig a one-man bunker, deep and long enough to sleep in it. Gates and I built ours a few feet from each other. The ground was hard and it made it harder to dig without proper tools. Once again, we had fucked up: we had forgotten our E-tool for digging. We used our knives and anything shiny we could find to get the trench dug.

The second lieutenant called for us to see him ASAP. He finally briefed us on the operation and what was expected of us. We were on a full regiment search-and-destroy operation. Our platoon was the central operation command for 1st Battalion, 5th Marines. The letter companies, Alpha, Bravo, Charlie, and Delta, where to our front. We wiremen, Lance Corporal Rivera and Gates, were there for security and to carry the radio relay antenna. The radio relay antenna was there for long-range radio communications. Gates and I just looked at each other, then stared at the bag holding the antenna, which held numerous aluminum tubes that, when hooked together, made an antenna. The antenna extended about twenty feet with a base and guidclines to keep it straight up. It was only several pounds and the bag had a carrying strap, but it was difficult to carry. Gates and I took turns carrying the bag that held the antenna. The antenna was never put up to communicate. It sure tired the hell out of Gates and me.

That first night at the banana plantation, after the brief, we returned to our sleeping quarters and heated up some C-rats for supper before sundown. The order for night was no lights or smoking after sundown. Charlie knew that we were there. About midnight the shit hit the fan! We got rained on by rockets and mortars. Instead of sleeping in our trenches, we were sleeping next to them. As soon as the incoming started, it was pitch-black and I had no sense of direction. So I started crawling with my rifle, looking for the trench I had dug. During that wild crawling frenzy I crawled over Gates. Gates got all pissed off that I woke him up and later he thanked me. He said that he was so fucking tired that if I had not crawled over him, he might not have woken up. I didn't give him a you're-welcome; I just yelled, "Let's find and get in our holes!" It seemed like hours but it had only been a minute or so before we located our trenches.

Old Charlie kept the rockets and mortars coming in all morning. The call for a corpsman ("Corpsman-up!") was the only other noise heard that morning. Every time a rocket or mortar hit a light broke the darkness. I could hear the shrapnel cutting through the banana trees and their branches. Just as suddenly as it had started, it stopped. We just fell asleep where we lay and hugged Mother Earth. Later on the wounded were medevaced out by helicopter. Our platoon commander insisted that we render a salute. We gladly obliged.

Sometimes we went out of our way to salute him. Someone wise him to the salute and his Lieutenant Bank.[A24] A day later he passed the word to stop the salute and his ___ [A25] were not visible. The second lieutenant was learning fast that this was not Quantico. I recall that he asked me to get an E-tool and dig a shitter for him. I just looked at him and started laughing and walked away. As I walked away, I muttered to myself, "Yeah right."

We spent several days at the banana plantation and then the move started. We normally walked about half the day and sometimes we walked at night. We always walked in a column with about ten feet between each other. We walked in a circle out of An Hoa and later we started heading away from An Hoa into Arizona Valley. About noon on the first day we stopped for the day. An Hoa was behind us and a forest of mesquite trees and brush was to our front. We were informed that a small river was between us and An Hoa. We asked permission to bathe in it. Since it was in sight distance, we were given the green light. So four of us with towels and soap took the opportunity and went. The water was dark and looked dirty but we thought that with a little soap we could get some of the dirt off. While two took to the water the other two stood guard. We even washed the clothes we had on and let some of them dry on our person. It was a lazy afternoon; most of us just took the opportunity to rest.

Gates and I went to ask about security watch for the night and we were informed that there would be none, that we were moving out at sundown. Just as the sun set we got the orders to settle up. It was made clear that we were to walk in a single column, ten feet apart. Also to ensure that we kept within eye contact of the Marine in front of us and that if for any reason we got lost, to just stay put and someone would come back for us. We were also told that if we came to any clearing to run across it, because at night we cast a big shadow. It was a bitch, but I never lost sight of the Marine in front of me. And what made it more difficult to hide was that flares kept being shot off and that created a bigger shadow. Every time I came to a clearing and I ran across it, I would cast a hell of a shadow.

The night was scary but fun; walk and run, keep your fellow Marine in sight or die. The mesquite trees had very sharp needles. When I was a kid, I played in a mesquite forest. I almost felt at home. Also on the mission I found some chili plants. Yes, I picked what the plant had! I ate green jalapeno chilis for a while. I guess if it wasn't for the war, Vietnam would have been a nice place.

As we marched, I kept on running into stickers. So I kept to the middle of the trail. And about midnight, we got ambushed. As soon as the first round went out, I was hugging the ground. I just lay there waiting for orders. In the meantime, I lay there in pain. The mesquite needle-nose stickers had pierced my hands! It hurt like hell but the will to live was greater. In my mind I either had to take the pain or get shot. After what seemed like hours but had only been minutes, a whisper came down the line that all was clear and to continue walking. I pulled out a small branch of stickers and continued on. A few minutes later the platoon stopped and we made camp. Now came the fucking rain! In the rain the poncho was your best friend. Everyone else was also trying to rest a little.

I woke up to a foggy morning and no mesquite trees. I sat up and could not believe what I was seeing. This was the area where some of the incoming fire had hit earlier this morning. A fire mission had been called on the area. There were half-burnt trees, some of the stumps still smoldering, and the combination of fog and forest made it look scary. Charlie had left in such a hurry that they'd buried their dead in hastily constructed graves. The rain had stopped but the smell of burned dead bodies was strong. It was time to move.

We, as command and control, stayed in the middle of Battalion Infantry Company Unit. We just slipped on by and the days just mirrored each other. As we walked and camped through Arizona Valley we endured numerous ambushes. In those three months we had numerous deaths. All you could do was thank the Lord that you were OK for now!

I met Mr. and Mrs. Leech on an ambush. We had been walking on rice-paddy dikes for most of that afternoon when small-arms and machine-gun fire opened up on us from the right. It was my turn to carry the radio relay antenna bag, so when I dropped the weight carried me to the right. I was partially submerged in the rice-paddy water. I just kept my head up to get my bearings. A loud voice shouted for us to get on line and walk out of the rice paddy. We were only about twenty yards out but it seemed like forever! On the way out I hit a hole and I went underwater. The heavy load kept me down. Thank God the other Marine next to me was taller than I. He pulled me out of the hole and helped me carry the bag. As soon as we came out I was pulling leeches off of me and thanking him for his help. My partner Gates came over and helped with the leeches. We had to burn some of them off.

Gates was several Marines behind me so he had a better view of the ambush. He asked if I was OK. I told him that I was good but that rice-paddy hole had almost caused me to drown. Not that, he said, the rounds that were hitting my head.

I had heard the firing but I didn't know or see where the rounds were hitting. Gates said that the machine-gun rounds were hitting by my head. I just said, "Fuck!" I told him that I hadn't seen or felt the rounds hit next to me!

Now that we were all wet, we settled for the day and night. We made camp and allowed our clothes to dry.

There were some times while I was walking that my knees wanted to buckle on me. I felt like I could not take another step, but the urge to live was greater.

On one of our rest stops a colonel joined us! When he came in, we thought the chopper was dropping off some supplies. He was fresh off Stateside duty, so he wanted to see what his battalion was doing. I guess he thought that he was back in Camp Pendleton.

We were woken up before sunup and started on a forced march. We were told that the colonel had ordered the march. He was going to show us how to get from point A to point B. We force-marched from sunup to sundown with ten-minutes rests. Numerous things happened that day: we were led by a colonel, walked all day, and had our first casualty.

I was about in the middle of the column. In front of us I could see several hills and as I got to the base of the first hill, we got ambushed. Mortars started hitting all around me. I am surprised that none of the shrapnel hit me. I could see the mortars exploding in front of and on both sides of me. I heard a loud yell to hit the high ground. Now, I had a board pack on my back. It had a quick-release lever, so I pulled and dropped the pack and started up the hill. I heard what I hadn't heard in a long while: "Corpsman-up!" It was then that I realized that Charlie was walking the mortars on our column.

I finally reached the top and the platoon sergeant asked me if I was OK. I said yes but that I had left my board pack at the bottom of the hill. He asked me to go and get it. I said, "Yes, but let me do it later or in the morning." I reminded him that it was still a hot zone down there. Before I got an answer, Gates ran down and got it for me. He had more balls than sense.

The word spread fast that the casualty was our radio operator. I wish I could recall his name but I can't. He got hit by just one piece of shrapnel, but it hit in the throat area and killed him. He only had a week to go but he chose to spend it with us in the field! We all got to know him very well. He was engaged to get married, and the wedding was supposed to be the following month. A day didn't go by that he didn't tell us about his plans and show us the picture of his future wife. As for the colonel, the gossip went that upon his return to the headquarters, he was relieved of his duties as the commanding officer. He could also have been promoted, but that's how the gossip traveled about why the colonel was no longer with the 5th Marines. I guess that was the way that we justified our friend's death.

It felt like as soon as we felt comfortable in one area, we moved to another. It was pretty peaceful for a couple of weeks. We were finally out of the rice paddies and into jungle. We were on a search-and-destroy mission, or a mop-up. So everything had to be either dead or gone. While we were camped in a wooded area we ran into an old Vietnamese mamasan, an old lady. She come right into our camp and asked for food. She talked and smiled at us. She the guy played tricks on her and left about it. [A26] Now that I looked back on that, it seems odd. No one questioned why she was there. There was no village nearby that I recall. I guess it's one of those things that happens that has no rhyme or reason. This forested area resembled Sequoia National Forest. The Sequoia National Forest was where I camped as a Boy Scout. I loved the fun that we had and the games that we played.

We moved deeper into the jungle and at a slower pace. We had been pretty lucky so far, only one casualty. Infantry squad were always close by and now even more so, because we were advised that the commanding officer was stopping by to say his goodbyes! His tour of duty was up. We had not seen him since we'd had the command center outside of Phu Bai, three months prior. He was coming in with the supply drop.

As the chopper was coming it started to receive small-arms fire. One of the nearby squads must have silenced the attacks, because after a short firefight, the firing stopped and the chopper landed. The colonel said his goodbyes while we were unloading the chopper. All of a sudden we started receiving small-arms fire again. Most of the supplies had been unloaded except for five-gallon containers of fresh water. So I and another Marine took our utility shirts off for quicker movement. We let another Marine hold our rifles and we just ran back and forth to the chopper and took out the containers. It was just a quick reaction on our part. The chopper had to be unloaded, and quick. We just hoped that neither one of us got hit. The colonel must have done a quick hello and goodbye because suddenly there he was, hugging the side of the gully, waiting to return to the chopper. I just looked at him and smiled. I don't know if he noticed me or not. He looked pretty tense and a little worried. We set up a field of fire where the incoming fire was coming from and the colonel boarded the chopper and off he went.

We stayed in that area for about a week. Steve Gates and I had dug our own personal bunkers. It was just a hold we could lie down in. We had snapped our two ponchos together to make a two-man tent. The small trenches were right outside the tent. A small trail and hedges ran a few feet from our camp. We were getting pretty comfortable and a little careless. And at midday we got hit. Small-arms and machine-gun fire opened up on us. I crawled to my trench and Gates seemed lost. I yelled at him and told him to stay put. But he didn't have his rifle. It happened so fast that he'd crawled into his trench without his rifle.

The firing was coming from the other side of the hedges. The rounds were hitting a few inches above us so that if we had half-raised our arm it would have been shot off. There was Gates crawling to get his rifle. He finally recovered it and crawled back to his trench. I thought I was going to have a dead friend. We were pinned down so that we couldn't return fire. Lucky for us that a squad nearby came and saved our bacon. My eyes were glued to the hedges waiting to start firing as soon as they came through them. We didn't even have time to get scared. Gates and I had a few words. I told Gates that what he did was stupid and that he should have listened and stayed put. All he said was, "If I am going to die I am going to die firing my rifle." We were still alive; there wasn't anything else to say.

On the following morning we policed the area and followed the trail that ran next to where we had been camped. We walked in a staggered column ten feet apart. We encountered numerous booby traps. But thanks to good point men, the booby traps were found and compromised. The jungle brush got thick and the only noise that could be heard was our bodies moving through the foliage. I was starting to get a little tired, but then the sound of several rounds could be heard coming from a distance and the familiar sound made me forget all about being tired. Again about five rapid shots and some return fire broke the silence. I went to my knee and the column stopped. We looked around and we looked at each other without saying a damn thing. Minutes later two Marines were being carried back in ponchos. As they were carried by me, I could see where the bullets had entered their bodies. One had two entry holes in the side and the other in about the same area. We continued on our way. We finally stopped and made camp for the night and some of us thought they'd been killed by a sniper. But just the same, we'd lost two Marines. I recall looking at their wounds and their facial features and thinking to myself that they looked at peace. It was like if they were saying, "Thank you, no more suffering for me."

Finally, in the middle of August, Steve Gates and I were informed that a relief was being brought in for both of us. It felt like Christmas and I felt like I had been given the best present ever. A few days later another wireman came in to replace both of us.

We were scheduled to return on the next supply chopper. We were directed to the landing zone to wait. We didn't say much to each other; we just kept looking back. There were a few more Marines waiting to return to base. All we could do was wait. A prisoner was brought in to be returned to base for interrogation. He was tied up and blindfolded and he posed no danger. However, a few Marines took it upon themselves to fuck with the prisoner. Apparently a sniper had just killed one of their squad members and this was their way of coping with his death. While the prisoner was sitting, a canteen was shaken in front of his face, the canteen was placed in front of his mouth, and when he reached to take a drink, the canteen was tilted and the water spilled to the ground. We just stared in disbelief. The prisoner also had an old wound in his forearm and peanut butter from one of the C-ration cans was spread on the wound. I don't think the prisoner felt the peanut butter on his forearm because it looked like gangrene had already set in. These two Marines seemed to be enjoying the moment! And finally a gunny came over and told them to stop the bullshit and leave the prisoner alone. All this happened in a matter of minutes and then the sound of a chopper broke the air. Smoke was tossed to spot the landing zone for the chopper.

It felt good to get out of the jungle. It was nice to eat hot food again. There was limited work for a wireman. We were scheduled for troubleshooting, security, and night patrol. But a week later I was volunteered to work at the West Pack central command headquarters. A switchboard was set up within the tent and the tent was well protected. We were given an access badge; there was a security guard checking for access authorization and concertina wire was constructed around the large tent. We worked eight on and eight off, 24/7. None of us switchboard operators knew each other and there was very little social interaction. I have never discussed with anyone the temporary duty (TAD) at the command center. Anyway, it was just work; besides, everything that was going on there was way above my pay grade.

It was nice to be back in An Hoa in the rear with the gear. I met up with two of my partners from home, Art Renteria and Rudy Castillo. Art and I had joined the Corps on a buddy system. The buddy program was just another way to recruit two instead of one. Art had gone to motor-transportation school (Motor-T) and become a truck driver. I had just finished eating lunch when I heard a familiar voice calling my name. As sure as hell there was Art, sitting in a big-ass truck. He was part of a convoy that had dropped supplies to us and the convoy was on its way back. We just had a few minutes to shake hands, wish each other well, and he was gone. He did inform me that another friend of ours was here with 11th Marines, Rudy. 11th Marines was the supporting artillery unit for 5th Marines. I visited with Rudy whenever I could.

Here in An Hoa I lost more friends. An Hoa was like a small city, but the danger was not within; the danger came from outside of the compound. We had manned watchtowers, bunkers, and concertina wire all around. We got periodic incoming mortar and sniper fire that reminded us that Charlie was still out wanting to kill us. 5th Marines Infantry Unit were constantly in the field fighting Charlie.

Night patrols took a lot of lives but that was a way for us to keep Charlie at bay. The night-patrol duty was shared by all the units left. I don't know if being out in the brush is more dangerous than staying in the rear. The night patrols would leave at sundown, set up a night ambush, and return at sunup. I met a Marine from Fresno and we happened to be the same age. We used to talk about home and family. We were planning on getting together in Fresno and partying. We were going to go to every bar in town and do some serious celebration. We both turned twenty-one in Vietnam and now we were old enough to go into a bar. Then the night patrol that he was with was ambushed on its way back. He was the only casualty. A piece of shrapnel from a mortar round hit his throat area and killed him. If the shrapnel would have hit him anywhere else, it would have been a flesh wound. His picture hangs at the Museum of Valor in Fresno, California.

I also lost another friend on another night patrol. I requested to take his place on this particular patrol. It happened that it was wire section's turn to provide a body for the night patrol. I wanted to be that person. The platoon sergeant denied my request. I pleaded with him not to volunteer him. I just had that gut feeling that something was going to happen to him. I tried to explain to the sergeant that he was, "Too gung ho" and too good of a Marine for his own good. But he wouldn't hear of it, and nothing was going to change his mind. I said my goodbye and I don't even remember what else I said to him.

On the following morning I went out to wait for the night patrol to come in. He wasn't among the patrol. It felt like someone had reached in and pulled my heart out. I questioned the squad leader and he told me that they set an ambush and double-timed coming back and that one minute he was there and the next he was gone. They believed that he must have gotten lost. His radio in a report [A29] and another patrol was going out to look for him. He was never recovered. How can you lose a six-four Marine? I went back to our area unit and I confronted the sergeant and all I could say was, "I fucking told you, I fucking told you!"

The reason that led to a certain Marine being singled out was wrong and, in my opinion, childish and unbecoming of a Marine. The night before one of us wiremen was going to be assigned night-patrol duty, we'd had a bullshit session, if you will. After a long day of work we would sit outside our tent and say whatever came to our mind. It was about ninety-nine percent bullshit talk, nothing serious. However, on that evening the bullshit got heated, but most didn't think much about it. Talk was all in fun; there was no rank, only Marines talking nonsense. I recall the sarge telling my partner, "Fuck you," and my partner telling the sarge, "Fuck you." Eventually my partner told the sarge, "Fuck you and your family." We were all laughing and the sarge took off, pissed. I believe the sarge took it personally and this was his payback! I ran into the sarge about twelve years later and told him that I blamed him for his death. If he ever reads my story, I hope that he accepts my apology. It was war and shit happens in war.

There were many useless deaths in the war. When I first arrived in country, a Marine took revenge on another Marine and place C-4 explosives under his rack. Another Marine threw C-4 into the river with a fuse to witness the explosion. As he threw it it blew and killed him. He had only been in country two weeks.

One particular incident for which I can't seem to find a reasonable explanation is this. We were sent out to troubleshoot communication lines on Highway One bridges. I was tasked with this duty several times. On one of these occasions, a Marine struck up a conversation with me. He said that he was on security watch. The VC liked to transfer weapons and rise [A30] back and forth on the rivers. A squad stood guard on and around the bridge. He seemed to like it because he didn't have to be out looking for Charlie. He asked me if I wanted some pictures for souvenirs. Fuck yes. I thought they were going to be pictures of the local area and locals. He looked around, gave them to me, and told me to hide them. What the fuck! I don't know what made me do that but I didn't. I mailed them to myself. I mailed a separate letter to my mother, telling her about the large manila envelope that I had mailed to myself and to just put it away for me. Also under no circumstances to open it! I don't know why I did that but I did it. My mother never said a word about the envelope and I was ashamed and scared to ask her. The pictures were eight-by-eleven color pictures of dead Viet Cong. Someone had taken the time to mutilate them; some had broom handles or sticks stuck in their balls area, their stomach, head, and some I don't recall. I have no idea what became of those pictures, or what that Marine did with the picture he had, or of whom or when or where they were taken. Most important, why they were taken. Those images have been in my mind and I can't get them out.

When I first arrived in Vietnam and reported to 1st Battalion, 5th Marines, communications platoon, wire, there fifteen wiremen. After ten months there were ten of us wiremen left. We'd had most of the wounded at Phu Loc at the start of Tet, in February. In Phu Loc there were four wiremen wounded plus our communications platoon commander, Captain Duncan. Three of the wiremen wounded, as well as Captain Duncan, did return to us. Now here in An Hoa we had one killed in action. Our work as wiremen was limited; some of the wiremen were on temporary duty to other units. Once we set up a switchboard and ran communication lines on the perimeter bunkers and the 5th Marines headquarters offices, the work was done. Now a standard switchboard watch, troubleshoot, and night patrol left us with time on our hands.

The days were hot and sweaty but that did not keep us from doing stupid shit. A couple of wiremen decide to challenge each other to a boxing match. One thought he was Muhammad Ali and the other thought he was the Great White Hope. They squared off and started swinging at each other. But I don't recall if they ever actually hit each other. They looked like a couple of Ed Sullivan boxers jumping up and down for about thirty minutes or so. Eventually they stopped but kept on talking shit at each other.

One of the dumbest things we did was climb a fifty-foot telephone pole. The combat engineers had placed a few on the base with the intention of running communication wire or electrical wire but someone put a stop to that idea. The telephone pole looked nice and straight so we thought we'd have a race. It was not as if someone was going to get a prize for climbing it. I don't know why or who thought of it.

But the rules were simple: no strap belt, only gaffs and gloves. Four of us wiremen took the challenge. Two wiremen went about halfway and stopped and came down. But two of us made it all the way to the top, touched the top of the pole, and came down. Someone was keeping time but I don't recall which one of us had the fastest time. But what made this contest dangerous and stupid was that a sniper could have shot us or we could have gaffed out and hurt or killed ourselves. However, climbing that telephone pole felt good and I could, I would, do it all over again.

October was here and the Viet Cong was starting to pick up its activities. We were about to lose another wireman, except this time it was because Big Red's tour was over and he was going home, back to the world. It was only fitting that he go home with a bang. The party was well organized and held in the most secure place in the base, the switchboard bunker. He kept us together, he was our leader, and he was leaving us. Little Red came out of the bush to say his goodbyes. They were both from the same town, and both were Irish, with red hair and freckles. It just so happened that one was smaller than the other, and the names Little Red and Big Red stuck. We had a shortage of field radiomen. The wireman was tasked with filling the position. The wireman filled whatever billet he was tasked to fill. This night was a night to remember. I am sure that Big Red, wherever he's at, remembers. He recorded the happenings to remember all of us that spent a lifetime with him. We all gave him a little of us. Big Ponch and I sang "La Cucaracha," a Mexican song. Some hit on cans to simulate bongos, just singing whatever came into their minds. We talked about home and for that night it was Big Red's night. Little Red couldn't forget where he was. He had a finger of a Viet Cong in a small glass tube with alcohol. He didn't say where or how he got it but we knew. He took the glass tube with the finger out and he would laugh with an uncontrollable laugh. We were all a little crazy, so it was natural to act crazy, if you will. As a combat radioman he was in the middle of the action, 24/7.

I don't know how long the party lasted, because when I left it was still going strong. It was so pitch-black outside that it took me about twenty minutes to get to my tent, when it should have only taken me four minutes. As soon as I stepped outside the bunker, I stopped and I felt alone and lost. I walked in the direction that I thought my tent was located in. I could hear occasional fire but no sustained firing. I would close and open my eyes but nothing changed; it was still pitch-black. I heard a faint pop; a parachute flare went off, some distance away from the base. But it created enough light that it allowed me to see the silhouette of my tent. The tent was only about ten feet from me. I must have been walking in circles. I found my rack and I just threw myself on it and thought of what had just happened and the party for Big Red. I felt sad and happy at the same time. I lay there thinking of how I was going to miss that freckled face and smile of Big Red. And about how two months out in this bush had changed Little Red.

I also wondered if anyone was going to collect the bounty that was placed on an officer's head. One of the companies while out in the field had lost most of its Marines. The way the story was told was that the company commander ordered his platoon to attack a hill and that within a week the company had been reduced to combat strength of less than one platoon[A31] . The platoon commander put more value on the hill than on his Marines. So a bounty was placed on his head. It might have been just talk, I don't know. War makes some of us crazy and callous. In the morning everyone was up and about, watching Big Red climb on a helicopter that was going to take him to Danang and home.

Our wireman hooch—our tent, which was our living quarters—was right next to the sick bay. The sick bay tent was the doctor's office, if you will. Sick call took place every morning. Since there were no house calls, if you happened to take ill, you would have to wait until the morning. However, in case of attack, a fortified bunker had been built in the middle of the base. Encounters with Viet Cong were becoming a daily occurrence. 11th Marines, our artillery support unit, was being kept pretty busy. It wasn't unusual to hear the artillery firing, fire mission. It was starting to resemble Phu Loc. One of those Vietnam mornings a couple of us were heading for some breakfast and a sick-bay line had already formed. All of a sudden the artillery unit began a fire mission and someone on sick-bay line dropped to the ground and started kicking and crying. We looked over to see who he was. He was a Navy corpsman. We commented to the corpsman that came to take care of him that he must have seen a lot of action as a corpsman with the grunts. The corpsman commented that he didn't know why he broke down, because he was new and he was in the process of checking in. You never know what causes a person to break down. I still don't know what caused me to break down the first time I came under fire.

In October the Viet Cong kept proving [A32] our perimeter and on occasion they would drop a mortar or two. The days were were still hot and muggy. We had community showers that were constructed by the Navy Seabees and this was our heat relief. A shower also gave me the opportunity to wash my clothes.

As I showered I washed all my clothes, and after the shower I put my clean clothes back on. So by the time I returned to my hooch, my clothes had dried on me.

A strange thing happened: the sarge called for a meeting, not a formation, and he assigned duty assignment for the night. Usually duties were scheduled by the week. Looking back, we should have guessed that something was expected to happen, or at the very least we should have been warned. The sarge assigned me as the night troubleshooter with him. I was on call to repair any communication line that happened to go down. He told me to relax. The night was extremely dark and spookily silent. I couldn't stand still; I was hoping that a break in communication would happen so I could go out. I finally gave in to comfort. I took my boots off and relaxed. I just lay there waiting and carrying on a conversation with the sarge.

Then all I could mutter was, "Oh fuck, we are under attack." All hell broke loose. The Viet Cong hit us with small-arms, machine-gun, and mortar fire. I bent down to put my boots on. The sarge yelled, "Let's get the fuck out of here!" Several mortars landed on our hooch. The sarge yelled, "I am hit on my lip and I am hit on my arm." We ran for the medical bunker. Mortars were hitting everywhere. We were being overrun. We ran from hooch to hooch, using them as protection. We would wait until the mortars stopped coming into the area in front of us and then we'd run to the next clear hooch. We could hear continuous firing everywhere.

All this time my arm kept on bleeding. But bleeding was the least of my problems; I needed to get to the medical bunker without getting killed. I don't know what Sergeant Bart was thinking, but I am certain that was his thought too. Bart stopped and told me, "We made it," and pointed to a bunker fortified with sandbags. The bunker was only about ten yards away but we waited until the sound of incoming mortars moved away and then made a run for it. Someone was guiding our path, because mortar rounds were exploding everywhere and we didn't get a scratch.

A Navy corpsman attended to my wound. He cleaned off the blood, but he could not stop the bleeding, so he pulled several veins together and tied them. He asked me if this was my first and I told him no. He said, "You are going home!" I lost sight of Bart the sarge. I must have fallen asleep, because when I opened my eyes it was light. I was instructed to return later for evaluation.

The hardest hit area was the back gate. The Viet Cong had rammed the gate with a truck but were stopped and killed. Most of that area was destroyed. I wanted to go find Rudy, my homie, but I needed to report back to my unit. I reported back but I couldn't find Bart. My arm started fucking hurting, so I took it out of the sling, but it felt stiff. My arm had swelled. I walked back to the sick bay and showed them my arm. The wound had gotten infected. The corpsman gave the infection a name but I can't recall it.

A medevac was called for me. I was immediately taken to the runway and placed on a chopper and transported to a Danang hospital. I had heard about the helicopter the Cobra and its combat and speed capabilities. But here I was getting medevacked on one. I was strapped on the right side of the Cobra and off we went. Everything that I recall about the Cobra was true. It was traveling at treeline level at about one hundred-plus miles an hour. As I lay there, I kept looking at the treeline in amazement and thinking to myself that I was open for a sniper to take a shot at me.

I was placed on antibiotics and informed that there were numerous shrapnel fragments in my arm. The hospital was made of several structures separated according to the seriousness of the patient's need. My wound was not serious but the infection had made it serious. It had to heal inside out, no stitches.

Two weeks later I was on my way back to An Hoa. I reported back and I was informed that I had orders. I was given until the following day to check out. I had time to check out and say my goodbyes. My first stop was Rudy at 11th Marines. All he said was, "You going to fucking leave me here, Little Joe?" We sat there and finally he got the fuck out of there. I gave him a big bear hug, turned, and left[A33] !

All around An Hoa there continued firefights. The following morning, I picked up my orders and boarded a chopper to Danang. As the chopper was flying out there were continuous fights. Small-arms fire, machine-gun fire, and mortar fire echoed through the area.

I took my last look at An Hoa with mixed feelings. I was leaving a family that I would never see again.

Awards

(1) 400 POINT PHYSICAL FITNESS CLUB CERTIFICATE
    LETTER
(2) USMC – MCRD SAN DIEGO CERTIFICATE SEP 2 1967
(3) NAVY ACHIEVEMENT W/ COMBAT "V" CITATION
(4) NAVY ACHIEVEMENT W/ COMBAT "V" CERTIFICATE

Photographs of the Republic of South Vietnam
1967–1968

Area

A. An Hoa – 1st Battalion, 5th Marines Camp
B. Danang
C. Hue City – Tet Offensive, 1968
D. Highway One
E. Camp Pendleton, CA, Infantry Training Regiment (ITR).
   Photo taken by Cpl. Art Renteria, USMC
   Motor – Transport – 11th Marines
   Motor – T Driver

*1966 Reedley College. This was the year before I enlisted. I was earning my
high school diploma at night while I attended community college to wrestle.
I ranked 2nd in state that year.*

STORY TWO

Summer of '67
A Chicano's Story

By

Joe T. Rivera

During the hot summer month of June 1967, Chico and I were contemplating enlisting in the military. We wanted out of the valley and out of working in the fields. As long as we could remember, it was the same routine: school, pick oranges, school, pick peaches, school, pick grapes, school, pick tomatoes or lemons or olives, and there seemed to be no end to it.

"You know what, Chico? There is no end to this madness; we have to just get the fuck out and enlist. Well, Chico, do you think it's a good idea that we join the military?"

"Orale! Why not, José, let's do it. I sure don't want to pick grapes the rest of my life. Anyway, it's just too fucking hot to do anything except drink beer."

Living in the mighty San Joaquin Valley, a cold Coors was always good to calm the thirst brought on by the hot summer sun.

"But before we give our pendejo asses to the military, let's go to the river and see if we can pick up a couple of chavalas. Como le ves. Pos! Vamos. Oh shit! I just remembered, I don't have any money for gas or pisto."

"That's not a problem, José. I have a five spot to do the job. Bamonos, what the fuck are we waiting for."

"Chico, did the viejito give you any shit when you asked him to buy you the pisto?"

"Fuck no! But just the same I gave him the cambio para su wine. Drive slow, pendejo. I got your pendejo hanging cabron! Orale lla, take it easy, I am spilling my beer all over and that's a waste. Stop!"

"Parate, what the hell for, José?"

"Mira, look over there by the tree, it's Mary Lou and Diane, and they are looking good. Estan buenas para el hijo de mi mama!"

"Leave your mother out of this, José, you're going to panic as usual and not say a damn word to them. Finish your beer, maybe you'll get some courage."

"Fuck off, Chico."

"I am going to whistle to get their attention."

"Come over here. Yeah, you pendejas."

"Here they come, José!"

"Yeah, yeah. I see them. Ya parale, Chico. All I want to do is talk to Diane. Don't fuck it up for me, Chico. Mira Nomas que cosas hace Dios. They are walking to your window, Chico!"

"You called us, Chico? Si y no."

"I whistled but José is the one that called. Mira, José…here they are."

"Bueno, all right, I am coming out."

"Stay here, Mary Lou, José wants to talk to Diane."

"Well, José?"

"Don't look at me like that, Diane."

"How should I look at you? You have never talked to me before. You always just look at me and walk away without a word."

"I am talking now, so let's walk over by the tree so we can be alone."

"You smell like beer, José."

"I just had a couple of drinks, that's all. Anyway, Diane, I want you to be mine. I mean, will you be my girl?"

"I don't know. I don't really know you and there is someone else."

"Bueno, OK! OK! But you will think about it?"

"Yeah, yeah. OK, I'll think about it."

"Orale, José, bamanos."

"I have to go, Diane. Hasta luego!"

"Oh shit, que pendejo soy. I just don't have the words to tell her how much I love her. I love her so much it hurts. I can still smell her perfume and feel her lips on mine. I was a little busy with Mary Lou. So, aber cuentame, how did it go?"

"Calmantes montes, Chico. Let me tell you, Chico, she is crazy about me. Pero, bamanos, let's get the hell out of here."

"Don't take it out on me, José. You struck out, berda?"

"A la chingada with baseball, Chico. No more questions, let's have another beer. Después te cuento, I'll tell you later."

"Well, Diane, what did José want?"

"Nothing."

"What do you mean nada? He is always looking at you and finally had the huevos to call you and talk you. And you say that nothing happened."

"It's just that Pablo might hear about it and get mad."

"I am not going to tell him anything. Anyway, you're not going steady with Pablo anymore."

"I know, I know, Mary Lou. But I am all mixed up."

"Your secret is safe with me, Diane. Chico is coming to the dance Saturday and José will probably be with him."

"Pablo will probably be at the dance too."

"So what!"

"Como que, so what! Don't mix up, Mary Lou."

"Enough, basta."

"José, let's go to the park and check on parties for tonight."

"Yeah. But keep your eyes on the road. Shit, Chico, are you trying to kill us?"

"Take it easy, José, I have everything under control."

"It seems like we have been on the road for hours."

"Hey, look over there in the corner of the park, all the vatos seem rather excited. I wonder what's up y que paso. They are waving at us to go over. Pos. Vamos. Now to find a pinche parking place. There is no place to park."

"Fuck it. Just park anywhere."

"Fuck it, this is as good as any."

"So what's up?"

"Chico, José."

"What?"

"Joe is dead. He was killed in Vietnam a few days ago."

"No shit! How did it happen?"

"They say he stepped on a mine."

"Oh man! Oh man! It's hard to believe that he's gone. Shit, we just saw him a few months ago partying up a storm. All he talked about was the Marine Corps and how proud he was to be a Marine."

"Fuck, and look what it got him. His wake is Saturday."

"José?"

"What, Chico?"

"Fuck the dance Saturday, right?"

"Orale. Firme. Fuck the dance. Joe wa san will always be our camarada!"

"When are you vatos leaving for Vietnam?"

"Orale, Peanuts, don't rush us. We haven't even enlisted yet."

"Well, José, when should we enlist?"

"Whenever you are ready, Chico."

"Bueno, I'll pick you up next week and we will do it."

"Give me some more time to think about it, OK?"

"There isn't shit to think about, I'll be by to pick you up."

Joe was buried with all military honors. It seemed like a nightmare. A bad dream.

You're gone from this earth, but in my mind you will always exist, Joe, young chicano, young Marine. Mi amigo, mi camarada, my friend.

Two weeks later.

I already honked my horn six times. I wonder what the fuck is keeping José. I guess I'd better get out and get him.

"Orale, José. How many times do you want me to knock?"

"Chicano, Chico, esperate, I am coming. Bamonos, mira, Chico, I am not sure if I want to do this."

"What! Como que no! José, that's all we talked about doing throughout senior year. Now we have to do it for Joe."

"I know. I know."

"Antoses vamonos. Let's be on our way, José."

"All right, I'll check it out. Orale."

"Gracias, thanks for coming along, keeping me company, and being my friend."

"OK. OK. Basta. Ya vamonos, already."

"Do you remember how to get to the recruiter's office?"

"Don't you remember, Chico?"

"I remember. I remember. Como que no."

"Well, antonses get us there."

"OK. OK. No te aguites. José, do I make a right or a left on Van Ness?"

"Make a right, pendejo! After the next stop go up four blocks and make another right. There, there on the left is the City Hall."

"I see it. I see it. One block up is the post office, and the recruiter's office is on the fourth floor. It would seem that the U.S. Government would have free parking for us chingones that are planning to enlist in the Marines. But no, it's going to cost us a dime to park. Do you have a dime, José?"

"Yes. Park and let's get in there and get it over with."

"Orale, that's the way to talk, José."

"Pos vamonos, Chico. Man, look at all those batos entering the building. I wonder if they are all going to the same play that we are going to. Ya callate, José. Look, there."

"What?"

"The elevator."

"Yeah, I see it."

"Well, get in."

"All right, don't rush me. Shit, Chico, that was sure a fast ride. Everything is happening so quick. What the hell am I doing here? Pa que chingados bine!"

"Callate, José."

"OK. OK."

But I know I am going to get talked into joining the Marines. Man, I just have this funny feeling that something is going to happen. We have been planning this for a long time. I wonder what Chico is thinking.

Man, I sure hope José joins the Marines with me. Well, here goes nothing. "Hey, José, the Marines are holding the door open for us."

"Come. Come, gentlemen. The Marine Corps is looking for a few strong young men. Have a seat."

"We want to be Marines."

"You're in the right place. Sergeant Patrick will be right with you."

"Gentlemen, I am Sergeant Patrick."

"Well, Sarge, I am Chico and this is José, and we want to join up."

"Great, great, but first things first. First you'll have to fill out an application. It's no big thing, I'll just ask you a series of questions and you answer them. I will also need your high-school diploma, social security card and birth certificate, and your green card or citizenship papers. Now, that didn't take long, did it? And now..."

"Wait. Wait. Sarge, we want to join the Marines, but we only want to enlist for two years."

"Not a problem. But next we will have to go to the Armed Forces Entrance Examination Service, which is located on the other side of town. This is where you will take a written and physical examination. Now, is there anyone else that you can think of that is thinking of joining the military?"

"No, Sarge."

"No, Sarge, but what are we going to do in the Marines? I mean, what kind of work is there for us?"

"You can be whatever you want to be, but first, let's finish all the testing."

"Sarge, I always wanted to be a mechanic."

"And you, José?"

"I just want to enlist for two years, that's all."

"Two years is a very short time and for that reason a lot of your friends have enlisted for two years. As a matter of fact, Raul Espinoza, maybe you know him, he got the last two-year program we had."

"Raul is from the same high school but he graduated last year."

"Besides, three or four years is not very long for you, either and it's better for you. Look here, and there, and there. This is a list of names of people from your high school and other high schools around the county that have enlisted in the Marine Corps. Your name will be added to that list, is that great or what? Except for Espinoza, they all enlisted for three or four years."

"Sarge, how do we get to the place where you said we are to test? Our car is…"

"Oh! Don't worry about your car; the parking and the trip to AFEES is on the Marine Corps. So just leave your car there. Let's go, gentlemen."

"Chico, three years is all I want to enlist for."

"Yeah, yeah, that's all I want to enlist for, too. Sit back and relax, José."

"OK. OK. But, Sarge, I don't want to leave for the Marines now."

"I am glad that you brought that up, because we have an outstanding program where you can enlist now and leave later. Now, isn't that great?"

"Let's do it, Chico."

"Let's do it, José."

"Chico, I am not very good at taking tests."

"Neither am I, José."

"But I have a hard time remembering things."

"Just relax and whatever you can't remember, just ask me or just guess. Now, can you remember that, José?"

"Shit yeah!"

"So shut up and listen."

"Well, Sarge, we passed everything, does that mean that we are in the Marine Corps?"

"It sure does. As a matter of fact, let me give both of you an honorary card with your names on it that will signify that you are both Marines. But first there are a few more papers that you must sign. Now here are your cards. Remember, if anyone wants a card like yours, have them call me collect; my name and telephone number are on the the back."

"Orale. Hey, shit hot, thanks, Sarge. I wanted to be a Marine as long as I can remember, even when I couldn't speak English."

"Not me, Chico, not until now. Shit, what did I get into?"

"Well, men, let's get back to your car. Remember, be back here next month for your orders."

I wonder what José was thinking; he almost backed out of enlisting. He must think I tricked him into enlisting with me. Well, maybe I did. Fuck it, I sure am glad that we are together. He is sure a good friend.

"Chico, you haven't said nothing since we left."

"I have a lot of things on my mind, sorry."

"Orale, no problem."

"Here is home for you, José."

"Yeah, thanks, later."

"Listen, I'll talk to you later."

"Yeah, yeah, later."

A few days later we were cruising the boulevard and we ran into Art. Art was a crazy Mexican who nobody fucked with.

"Hey, pendejos, I heard that both of you joined the Marine Corps."

"Yes, we did, Art."

"I've been in the Marine Corps for a year and it sucks big time. If I were you, I would stay the fuck out."

"No, we can't. I mean, we want to be Marines. Besides, we have already enlisted."

"Man, don't you pendejos read that newspaper or watch TV? There are all kinds of guys getting killed in Vietnam."

"Hey, Art, leave us alone, OK?"

"All right, but don't forget I told you so."

"Shit, Chico, first my parents get on my case for enlisting and then my friends."

"Art is nobody's friend. Don't let what Art said bother you."

"OK."

"Just say to yourself: I am a Marine, a bad-ass chingon."

"But shit, Chico, we haven't even been to Marine boot camp! Wow, ay cabron. Who is that good-looking jaina looking my way? Damn, if it isn't Diane. Drive over there and stop, Chico."

"Esperate, wait, let me find a place to turn around."

"Slow down."

"OK. OK."

"Stop!"

"Hi."

"Hi. I've heard that you joined the Marines."

"Yeah, I sure did. Chico and I enlisted together."

"I didn't see you at the dance."

"I couldn't make it. But I wanted to be there. Let me make it up to you."

"What did you have in mind?"

"Get in, let's cruise and talk about it. What do you say, Chico?"

"Sure, como no. Mary Lou can sit in front with me and Diane can sit with you in the back seat."

"OK. But we have to let Chela and the girls know that we are leaving."

"All right. Hurry back."

"Nos aventamos! Puro playboys…"

"Chico, I sure hope I don't blow it with Diane."

"You worry too much."

"José, wake up and open the door for Diane."

"Oh, I am sorry, Diane, I didn't see you walk up. But you sure are looking good. I mean, you look very pretty."

"I know what you mean, José. Thanks."

"Orale, Chico. Let's go."

"José, it's your turn to drive."

"What! Why now? You never let me drive your car before."

"Well, I am letting you now! Besides, it's getting late, and Mary Lou and me need to spend some time in the back seat. We have a few things to talk about."

"What! All right. All right."

"José, I haven't heard a sound from Chico and Mary Lou and you haven't spoken to me in over an hour. You haven't told me when you are leaving for the Marines."

"No, I guess I haven't. We are leaving tomorrow morning."

"You are what?! Why didn't you tell me sooner? Or were you not planning on telling me?"

"Yes, I was planning on telling you, but I just forgot."

"It's late, take us home."

"I'll take Mary Lou home first."

"No."

"OK. I'll take you home first. I don't know what you are upset about."

"I am not upset. Mary Lou is spending the night at my house and besides, it's late. You do know where I live."

"Of course I do. I'll have you home in no time."

"Remember, my house is the second house on the left after you turn on 11th."

"I know. I know."

"José."

"What, Chico!"

"Stop."

"I am stopping."

"Well, turn the car off. I need a few minutes to say goodbye."

"Let's go in, Mary Lou. Mary Lou, let's go."

"Just a few more minutes, OK?"

"I am going in."

"Wait! Let me open the door for you, Diane. Don't go yet, please. Stay a few minutes. It's going to be a long time before we see each other again."

"José, you didn't talk to me for over an hour and you weren't going to tell me that you were leaving. Bye."

"But Diane! At least let me walk you to your door."

"No. I have to go. Adios. Mary Lou, are you coming?"

"I'll call you before I leave in the morning."

"Yeah…OK."

"OK. José, hop in. Let's go."

"Shit, Chico, what did I do wrong?"

"You didn't do nothing wrong, José. Asina son las viejas. That's the way some women are, that's all."

"Man, she sure looked good walking up those stairs mad.

"Oh, well, ni modo! Tomorrow is another day."

"I never thought that tomorrow was going to come so fast."

"No shit."

"I don't know if I am ready with what happened tonight and all."

"Calm down, José."

"How am I supposed to feel? Tomorrow we leave."

"Yeah, I understand. But remember, you are not going to be alone."

"My uncle is going to take us to AAFES. So be ready in the morning. We will honk twice for you."

"Yeah, OK."

"See you tomorrow."

"See you tomorrow."

At the Armed Forces Examination Center.

"Hey, Sarge, I thought you said we were in the Marines and we were just coming to pick up our orders."

"Yes, on both counts. It's just a standard small physical to ensure that you are still in good health."

"Chico?"

"Yeah?"

"This pure bullshit."

"I know, but we're here and we are not the only ones."

"Can you hear what he's saying?"

"I think he said that he is Sergeant Charles and that he wants us to listen and shut up."

"What is he saying now?"

"Shut up and listen!"

"When I call your name, step up and the corporal will hand you a document with your name on it. Make sure that your name is spelled correctly. Listen up! We don't have all day. Now, with the document in your right hand, follow the yellow arrow. Make sure that you stop at all stations."

"Shit, this is bull, Chico."

"You're telling me, I could be at the lake with Mary Lou. But no, here I am with this bunch of pendejos."

"So you finally agree with me, Chico."

"Shut up up there, and let's keep moving."

"Oh shit. Did I hear him right? I guess I did 'cause everybody is turning around and facing the wall. We are to do what?"

"Let's make it snappy, pull your shorts down, bend down, and now put your hands on your cheeks and open up for inspection. Now turn around. Now turn your head to the right and cough, and now to your left and cough."

"Chico, I thought we were joining the Marines!"

"Shut up, José!"

"There is no talking during the examination unless spoken to by the doctor, and that means you two on the right."

"I wonder what Chico thinks now, now that he has had his balls and butt checked."

"Hey, how did it go with you, Chico?"

"I don't want to talk about it."

"That makes two of us."

"All of you have met the mental qualifications and now you have met your final physical qualifications required by the armed forces. On behalf of the United States government, I welcome all of you to Uncle Sam's military service. Now everyone raise their right hand and repeat after me."

Man, this is crazy. It seems like only yesterday I was in school, fighting the classroom system by never raising my hand to answer questions. And today I raised my hand and swore to defend the Constitution of the United States with my life. Wow!

"José, what are you thinking about?"

"Nothing. What's that envelope that they gave you? Is that our orders? I see my name on it."

"It has both our names on it. It's our orders and they told me to carry it and guard it with my life until I hand it to a sergeant that is going to meet us in San Diego. Oh, yeah. And here are our one-way tickets on the next bus to San Diego."

"The bus depot is three miles away. And who's taking us there?"

"There is no one that can take us there. We are going to have to walk it. We can do it, José. We've walked farther than that. Fuck it. Let's go."

"I wonder what boot camp is going to be like, Chico."

"I don't know, José. But I've heard that boot camp is harder and tougher than picking oranges, tomatoes, and grapes put together."

"Ni modo, that's life."

"Bueno. Here goes nothing."

Cisneros and Me. US Hospital Ship: The Repose. February 1968

STORY THREE

The Breeze

The breeze is hot-n-clammy

as it hits upon my brown Mexican face

The fruit trees sway to and fro with

strength and pride

as the breeze hits upon my brown Mexican face

The grapes-n-tomatoes grow ripe and gleam

as the breeze hits upon my brown Mexican face

I work-n-slave this land

The sun's rays hit and burn my face

as the breeze hits upon my brown Mexican face

I work-n-work and yet I am told,

"That's not enough, work some more!"

as the breeze hits upon my brown Mexican face

Insecticide dust and grime collects upon my face

as the breeze hits upon my brown Mexican face

America! America! Can't you see that all

these breezes are killing!

– Joe T. Rivera

*Camargo, GTO, Mexico 2006. My Father Juan (left),
next to my aunt Candelaria and uncle Masimino.*

www.ingramcontent.com/pod-product-compliance
Lightning Source LLC
Chambersburg PA
CBHW071505030726

47593CB00003B/1153